Meditations
on
Hunting

Meditations on Hunting

by
José Ortega y Gasset

Artwork by
Brett Smith

Translated by
Howard B. Wescott

Introduction by
Paul Shepard

Foreword by
Datus Proper

Published by Wilderness Adventures Press, Inc.™
45 Buckskin Road
Belgrade, MT 59714
866-400-2012
website: www.wildadvpress.com
email: books@wildadvpress.com

Second Edition

Printed in Canada

Library of Congress Catalog Card Number: 95-61397

ISBN: 9-78193-209853-2   (1-932098-53-4)

Contents

Translator's Preface

José Ortega y Gasset, Spain's leading philosopher of the twentieth century, was born in Madrid on May 9, 1883. After receiving his doctorate in 1904 from the University of Madrid he spent two years, from 1905 to 1907, studying at the Universities of Leipzig, Berlin, and Marburg. In 1910 he was appointed to the chair of Metaphysics at the University of Madrid, a post he occupied until 1936.

Ortega began publishing in magazines and newspapers at the age of nineteen, and in 1914, at the age of thirty-one, he brought out his first book, *Meditations on Quijote*. Between 1916 and 1934 he produced eight volumes of essays under the title *El Espectador* (The Spectator); founded in 1923 the magazine *Revista de Occidente*; became a delegate to the Republican Chamber of Deputies (Cortes Constituyentes) in 1931. He left Spain in 1936 and lived successively in France, Holland, Argentina, and Portugal, returning to Spain in 1945. In 1948 he founded the Instituto de Humanidades in Madrid with the cooperation of Julián Marías, a leading interpreter of his work. Ortega lectured in the United States in 1949 and between 1949 and 1951 gave frequent lectures in Germany and Switzerland. In 1951 he was named Doctor *honoris causa* by the University of Glasgow. He died in Madrid on October 18, 1955.

For Ortega, life is the basic reality with which man must contend. This seems a trivial statement at worst and an obvious one at best, but the truth of it is in fact as complicated as it is incontestable. I should qualify the statement by pointing out that life is, for Ortega, not the only reality, nor is it necessarily the most important one. It is simply the primary reality: the one that each individual confronts first and the one that makes the most urgent demands on each of us. As Ortega points out in

Meditations on Hunting, life is given to us empty and we are therefore inexorably forced to choose, or create, a course of action in each of life's situations.

Since our instincts no longer plan our lives for us, and since we always, even when acting "irrationally," somehow account for what we do, creating an activity is reasoning in the face of life's emptiness and insecurity. Thus reasoning, either by choosing or creating, is synonymous with living. Ortega called this idea the doctrine of *vital reason* (also referred to as "historical" or "living" reason), and it brings us to the keystone of his philosophy, the statement, "*Yo soy yo y mi circunstancia,*"—"I am I and my surroundings." Life is the dynamic interchange between the individual and his surroundings, and his surroundings include his own emotional and intellectual responses to life's problems. Thus knowledge, for Ortega, is knowledge of how to act, knowledge of what to hold to, and pay attention to, in the face of life's demands.

It is not surprising then, that the drama of the hunt should interest a man whose philosophical stance is based on the drama of biographical life. He looks at hunting from the perspective of what that activity has demanded of a particular individual and what it has meant to him within the context of his life

Because Ortega's philosophical method is in part biographical, it must also be in part historical. To understand what an activity means to a modern man, we must consider what it has signified to men throughout history. Thus Ortega examines hunting as an activity that has had its own development, and considers what that activity has meant to men in the various stages of evolution. This examination takes into account whether those men hunted by necessity or by choice, but the distinction has little meaning in the long run, for men can choose to hunt even if they do not need to and can need to hunt even if they do not choose to.

Finally, Ortega seeks the nature of hunting in the activity itself, considering it in terms of its inherent goal, and taking into account the fact that hunting is an activity that occurs throughout almost the entire zoological scale. His explanation of the relationship between hunting and man's nature will be found in the text.

Meditations on Hunting was originally written in Lisbon in 1942, as a prologue to *Veinte Años de Caza Mayor* [Twenty Years a Big-Game Hunter] by Ortega's friend Edward, Count Yebes, which was published in Madrid in 1943. The prologue has been separately published three times in Spanish (1947, 1949, and 1960) and three times in German (1954, 1959, and 1966) and has also been translated into Dutch (1964) and Japanese (1966). This is its first appearance in English. In this version the references to the Count and to his book (except for a few quotations, which are credited in footnotes) have been removed, since they are not meaningful without the book at hand, nor does Ortega's discussion of hunting depend for its effectiveness on its relation to the work which occasioned it. Because Ortega's method is, in the last analysis, a critical one, much of his writing, essays, prologues, magazine and newspaper articles, and books—is based on other works. Indeed, *Meditations on Quijote*, the fundamental work in which he first establishes the doctrine of vital reason, takes its departure from Cervantes's masterpiece.

Many of Ortega's major works have been translated into English; those who may wish to read more of him can easily find English versions of *Meditations on Quijote, On Love, The Origin of Philosophy, What Is Philosophy?, Man and People, Man and Crisis, The Modern Theme, The Mission of the University, Concord and Liberty, The Revolt of the Masses*, and *The Dehumanization of Art*.

Howard B. Wescott
Department of Hispanic Studies
Smith College

Introduction

*E*merging from the Racquet and Tennis Club of New York, where as a guest I had been scanning books on hunting in the Club's library, I looked down Park Avenue with its towering, monolithic buildings, its patina of wealth and power highlighted by elegant corporate foyers and suave inhabitants, and I was wrenched from my subject. How trivial seemed hunting against this overwhelming impression of infinitely complex machinery! I felt a sense of absurdity. Could anything in this glut of human success be more utterly meaningless, except perhaps in some recondite, academic way, than reminiscences by old duck shooters and manuals for young falconers? What could contrast more with the country pursuits of a few wealthy sportsmen or even the prehistoric arts of the chase than this awesome street which epitomized the will of man. All of nature and its study seemed remote. Only a faint yellow stain in the air hinted at some underlying disorder and the cost of such an imperious civilization.

The earth and air are strained by man's dominance, and the bonds of man and nature are broken by the definition of history. Nor are those bonds ever self-evident. Scientific understanding of the interdependence of species has accumulated slowly with ecology's rather ponderous investigations of symbioses, successions and communities. A half-century's work has uncovered a principle: elaborate and stable flow patterns linking forms through food habits. Such food relations—the food chains and food webs—define evolutionary categories, curb and channel and separate ways of life. The lives of all creatures are shaped by the details of feeding, not only in their physical anatomy and chemistry but in the most precise aspects of form and behavior.

Among the biological characteristics of the human species is the specialization of some parts of the central nervous system for storing and transmitting information symbolically. The older views that mental and cultural life set man apart from nature or that it constituted a remission from evolutionary selection are challenged by recent anthropological work. Comparative studies of many different primates suggest parallels to the prehuman situation of our evolution and the steps by which social, intellectual and even ethical traits came into existence in an ecological context, associated with the human animal's niche and, more particularly, his place in Paleolithic food webs.

These studies are slowly delivering a picture of the human mind as an adaptation to the physical environment, to band, clan and tribal organization, to the division of labor in hunting and gathering, to long life and delayed maturity, to the ceremonial hunting of large, dangerous mammals living in herds in open country—in short, to an environment and a way of life, the life of the Pleistocene hunter.

Together with physical traits, these are perfections generated in a hunting-gathering milieu, shaped during 99 percent of human time. Natural selection has directly created the most subtle and delicate aspects of thought, passion and art. We have gradually accepted human hands and legs as those of a hunter. Now we are ready to find in our heads the mind of the hunter: the development of human memory as a connecting transformer between time and space, derived from the movement of hunter and gatherer through a landscape; the Dionysian moment of unity and freedom in ecstasy of intense release unknown to herbivores, based on the recognition of the perpetuation of life at the moment of the kill; the mental use of other species as metaphors for social perception, which is a mode of totemic transformation reaching to the heart of thought, yoked by our evolution to the richness of world life, ushered into consciousness by the magic of the taxonomies of the species system and the terminology of anatomy as revealed by the hunter as butcher.

These recent developments in bringing social and natural sciences together are astonishingly anticipated by José Ortega y Gasset in *Meditations on Hunting*. When Ortega calls the present-day poacher "municipal Paleolithic man" he does not mean that he is low and brutal. He has perceived by an almost incredible act of intuition into the thoughts of hunters he has known personally and from literature that the glory of man is a hunting heritage.

Ortega recognizes that the antiquity and universality of the hunt signify deep, positive traits in all living men. He knows that routine work and drudgery are an invention of civilization, degrading to the human spirit. He acknowledges the purposeful uselessness of hunting, the handicaps by which hunters always neutralize their technological advantage, so that the hunt is changed from what we commonly regard as strictly economic. He perceives the ecological importance of size relationships among the hunters and hunted, which is the fundamental factor determining the number of links in food chain systems. He spurns the deceptive substitutes for hunting truly. He ponders the behavior of prey and predator as necessary to each other and interlocking, and he knows that game cannot be saved. He speaks of the numbers of animals as related to their role in the prey-predator series. He sees that domesticated animals are degenerate. He affirms the hunting way of life by man as a combination of high technical ability and religious sophistication.

Throughout, Ortega avoids the implicit full-knowledge of the cliché that "Man is an animal, but something more than an animal, too." Instead, Ortega says, "Man has never really known what an animal is." In this he turns away from the orthodox Western attitude that the nature of animals is self-evident. That tradition condemns the carnivore and the act of killing as evil, and now and again it reaches to the Orient for its reverence for life. But Ortega knows that only the hunter confronts this question with full human dignity, beginning with an affirmation of his ecology rather than its denial.

His description of the hunter is seldom so abstract as I make it sound. One of the most attractive aspects of his essay is the description of the individual hunter in the field: his minding of the environment, the fluid quality of his attention, and the habits of alertness and acuity that link him in participation with all of creation.

The hunter's vision is itself a part of nature. His perception of the signs of passage and signals of events is continuous with those events. His eye roves across a landscape which is itself living. The hunter in man lives an eventful life, a present, sound-filled pulse which collectively is the dynamic, oral, traditional society, where the poet is historian and men are bound in myth and music to a generous and religious existence.

The static cornfield, the static steel towers on Park Avenue, the static nature of print itself are, in a way, paltry gains. Recent peoples are terrifyingly separated from the organic root, frozen in fear of the necessity of being consumed, sick in bodies and minds which have tragically outlasted the great Paleolithic religious institutions.

When men hunted as a way of life, work as we know it did not exist. Since then only those fortunate enough to be free from work have kept the vestiges of hunting traditions. The great privilege of men of leisure has been hunting (and so it is not surprising after all to find a library of hunting books on Park Avenue).

It is a mystery to me how Ortega arrived at so sure a footing. He did not live to see the golden days of African anthropology, with fossil men virtually springing from the earth like cicadas, or the scores of educated ape-watchers who have been finding kinship beyond their dreams in the jungles, or the bitter maturity of ecology, which was little more than an intuition before a decade of fallout from nuclear bomb testing triggered worldwide pollution-consciousness. Yet he anticipated with profound accuracy the direction and basic formulations of a discipline which does not yet exist, a true ecology of men.

Ortega has grasped that essential human nature is inseparable from the hunting and killing of animals and that from this comes the most advanced aspects of human behavior. Intelligence in our species is a highly specialized function by which natural selection built the hunter's capacity to plan on the intensely social foundation of primate ancestry. The emergence of such complex functions as the unconscious, of language, and of dreams are inextricably part of the Paleolithic. Ortega does not scorn but affirms that past. A view of man so humble in the scale of nature and so audacious in its challenge to the homocentrism of our traditional philosophy will not be easily accepted. Yet, like the idea of ecology—indeed, as part of ecology—it will in time reach out to all areas of concern and thought.

First, however, it must penetrate the husk of 5,000 years of civilized fear and hostility toward nature in general and hunter-gatherers in particular. Only when our culture accepts the needs of living men as shaped by a prehistory which is still urgent in them, communicated to each by his chromosomes, will we be ready to follow the lead of Ortega's *Meditations on Hunting*.

Paul Shepard
Visiting Professor of Environmental Perception
Dartmouth College

Foreword

A philosopher would have been superfluous, when I was growing up. Ancestors living and dead had already informed me that wild was best and that hunting was the way to go wild. Nature, meanwhile, had filled the woods with good things. A child did not need to understand what was happening—not unless it hit below the belt.

When it hit first, I was eleven years old and Mom was waking me early. A furbearer worth three dollars was poking around the barn, she said, so I ran barefoot onto frosty grass, carrying a .22 rifle. As I tried to aim, however, an outrageous thing happened: My knees began to tremble so violently that pajama pants dropped around skinny shanks. My shot missed, of course, but Mom did not laugh. She recognized my emotion as the real thing—what philosopher Ortega y Gasset calls "mystical agitation." Dad called it buck fever. I had heard about the disease but didn't know you could get it from a skunk. That was not many years back, as history goes, but the world today groans under twice as many people, few of whom know much about skunks or mystical agitation. Urban children are raised in virtual reality, believing that animals speak English. Those young people are hunters still, all of them, but they shoot with joysticks and develop what Ortega calls "a funny snobbery toward anything wild, man or animal."

We need guidance in this "rather stupid time," and Ortega's essays are the obvious source. He is the philosopher who has looked most deeply into the hunting instinct, of which the fishing instinct is part. Further, he writes with the clarity you would expect from an heir of Socrates and Plato (both of whom hunted, as he points out).

Mind you, philosophic simplicity is not what we are accustomed to in this age of hype. Where we are reticent and convoluted, Ortega is direct and elegant. He looks through our foliage with falcon eyes, and we squirm.

An American reader should be aware, moreover, that Ortega is not in the tradition of Thoreau and Leopold—the natural philosophers with whom I (and perhaps you) grew up.

Henry David Thoreau gave up hunting and fishing to pursue bigger game. He wanted a wife too, but gave up marriage, and read the world's great books, but "travelled a good deal in Concord" on foot. And yet the abstemious New Englander and the cosmopolitan Spaniard agreed on what hunting is about. As you read Ortega's essay on "Vacations from the Human Condition," keep in mind this passage from Thoreau's *Walden*:

> *As I came home through the woods with my string of fish, trailing my pole, it being now quite dark, I caught a glimpse of a woodchuck stealing across my path, and felt a strange thrill of savage delight, and was strongly tempted to seize and devour him raw; not that I was hungry then, except for that wildness which he represented. Once or twice, however, while I lived at the pond, I found myself ranging the woods like a half-starved hound, with a strange abandonment, seeking some kind of venison which I might devour, and no morsel could have been too savage for me.*

Aldo Leopold was the conservationist, naturalist, and ecologist who gave us "the land ethic." Leopold hunted "meat from God," and this is how he found it:

> *The dog, when he approaches the briars, looks around to make sure I am within gunshot. Reassured, he advances...wet nose screening a hundred scents for that one scent, the potential presence of which gives life and meaning to the whole landscape.*

Ortega stands in contrast. He is a student of human nature, not Mother Nature, and of the universal, not the local. His landscape is a

stage on which hunters play the lead. He does not look into the disper-
sion of seeds, like Thoreau, or give animals a habitat like Leopold. What
we get from Ortega is a hunter's ethic, which governs relations between
two individuals—human and prey—and is older than the land ethic by
thousands of years.

What seems remarkable is not that Ortega, Leopold, and Thoreau
came into the landscape from such different directions. Their starting
points were fixed by the cultures in which they grew up, and cultures
change. What does not change is nature—human nature and Mother
Nature. We can be sure of this because, when the classical philosopher
and the two natural philosophers go hunting, they find themselves on
exactly the same trail. You and I can therefore follow it in confidence.

The measure of a philosopher, I suppose, is his ability to be right over
time, and one of life's coincidences gave me a chance to measure Ortega.
He had published his *Meditations on Hunting* in Lisbon in 1942. My
work took me there years later. One autumn weekend, after beating a
good deal of Portuguese brush, I picked up these essays and found a pre-
scient passage:

> *In all revolutions, the first thing that the "people" have done*
> *was to jump over the fences of preserves or to tear them down, and*
> *in the name of social justice pursue the hare and the partridge.*
> *And this after the revolutionary newspapers, in their editorials, had*
> *for years and years been abusing the aristocrats for being so frivo-*
> *lous as to...spend their time hunting.*

And that was exactly what happened in Portugal after the revolution of
1974. While Communist leaders were still trying to tell the workers what
their struggle was about, they stuffed themselves, four at a time plus
dogs, into very small cars. There were traffic jams on the way to the
fields and lines of Fiats and Citroëns headed back to Lisbon after dark,
bearing hares and partridges and exhausted hunters. They were not expe-
rienced and not yet governed by a tight code of ethics, but they had made
a start at what they had always dreamed of doing.

It was what Ortega y Gasset had predicted three decades earlier. The
old regime might have diminished revolutionary fervor if it had listened

to the philosopher when he explained that hunting is not a "reasoned pursuit." On the contrary, he wrote, it is "however strangely, a deep and permanent yearning in the human condition.

And besides, no one who hunts all day has enough energy left to start a revolution.

Datus Proper
Belgrade, Montana

Hunting
as
"Diversion"

ust as the leaping stag tempts the hunter, the topic of hunt-
ing has often tempted me as a writer. My intention is to
try to clarify a little this occupation in which devoted
hunters engage with such scrupulousness, constancy, and
dedication. Just what kind of occupation is it?

In our time—which is a rather stupid time—hunting is not considered
a serious matter. It is thought that enough has been said on the subject by
calling it a diversion, presupposing, of course, that diversion, as such, is
not a serious matter. Yet serious examination should lead us to realize
how distasteful existence in the universe must be for a creature—man, for
example—who finds it essential to divert himself. To divert oneself is to
separate oneself temporarily from what one usually is, to change for a
while our usual personality for another which is more arbitrary, to
attempt to escape for a moment from our real world to others which are
not ours. Is this not strange? *From what* does man need to divert himself? *With what* does he succeed in diverting himself? This is not the
time to become involved in such provocative questions; I merely wanted
to point out in passing that the question of diversion brings us more
directly to the heart of the human condition than do those great melodra-
matic topics with which the demagogues berate us in their political
speeches.

At present, however, I am interested in underscoring a feature of hunting that runs contrary to what is usually understood by diversion. This
word, diversion, usually indicates only comfortable situations, to the
extent that, used carelessly, it connotes ways of life completely free of
hardship, free of risk, not requiring great physical effort nor a great deal

of concentration. But the occupation of hunting, as carried on by a good hunter, involves precisely all of those things. It is not a matter of his happening to go into the fields every once in a while with his rifle on his shoulder; rather, every good hunter has *dedicated* a part of his existence—it is unimportant how much—to hunting. Now this is a more serious matter. Diversion loses its passive character, its frivolous side, and becomes the height of activity. For the most active thing that a man can do is not simply to do something but to dedicate himself to doing it. Other living beings simply live. Man, on the other hand, is not given the option of simply living; he can and must dedicate himself to living— which is to say that he must hand over his life, or parts of it, deliberately and under his untransferable responsibility, to specific occupations. Dedication is the privilege and torment of our species. And it happens that many men of our time have dedicated themselves to the sport of hunting. Furthermore, throughout universal history, from Sumeria and Acadia, Assyria and the First Empire of Egypt, up until the present now unraveling, there have always been men, many men, from the most varied social conditions, who dedicated themselves to hunting out of pleasure, will, or affection. Seen from this point of view, in its authentic perspective, the topic of hunting expands until it attains enormous proportions. Consequently, aware that it is a more difficult matter than it seems at first, I ask myself, what the devil kind of occupation is this business of hunting?

Hunting
and
Happiness

he life that we are given has its minutes numbered, and in addition it is given to us empty. Whether we like it or not we have to fill it on our own; that is, we have to occupy it one way or another. Thus the essence of each life lies in its occupations. The animal is given not only life, but also an invariable repertory of conduct. Without his own intervention, his instincts have already decided what he is going to do and what he is going to avoid. Therefore, it cannot be said that the animal occupies himself with one thing or another. His life has never been empty, undetermined. But man is an animal who has lost his system of instincts or—which is the same thing—retains only instinctual stumps and residual elements incapable of imposing on him a plan of behavior. When he becomes aware of existence, he finds himself before a terrifying emptiness. He does not know what to do; he himself must invent his own tasks or occupations. If he could count on an infinity of time before him this would not matter very much: he could live doing whatever occurred to him, trying every imaginable occupation one after another. But—and this is the problem—life is brief and urgent; above all, it consists in rushing, and there is nothing for it but to choose one way of life to the exclusion of all others; to give up being one thing in order to be another; in short, to prefer some occupations to the rest. The very fact that our languages use the word "occupation" in this sense reveals that from ancient times, perhaps from the very beginning, man has seen his life as a "space" of time, which his actions, like bodies of matter unable to penetrate one another, continue to fill.

Along with life, of course, there is imposed upon us a long series of unavoidable necessities, which we must face unless we are to succumb. But the ways and means of meeting these have not been imposed, so that even in this process of the inevitable we must invent—each man for himself or drawing from customs and traditions—our own repertory of actions. Moreover, strictly speaking, to what extent are those so-called vital necessities really vital? They are imposed upon us to the extent that we want to endure, and we will not want to endure if we do not invent for our life a meaning, a charm, a flavor that in itself it does not have. This is the reason I say that life is given to us empty. In itself life is insipid, because it is a simple "being there." So, for man, existing becomes a poetic task, like the playwright's or the novelist's: that of inventing a plot for his existence, giving it a character which will make it both suggestive and appealing.

The fact is that for almost all men the major part of life consists of obligatory occupations, chores which they would never do out of choice. Since this fate is so ancient and so constant, it would seem that man should have learned to adapt himself to it and consequently to find it charming. But he does not seem to have done so. Although the constancy of the annoyance has hardened us a little, these occupations imposed by necessity continue to be difficult. They weigh upon our existence, mangling it, crushing it. In English such tasks are called "jobs"; in the Romance languages the terms for them derive from the Latin word *trepalitum*, which originally meant a terrible torture. And what most torments us about work is that by filling up our time it seems to take it from us; in other words, life used for work does not seem to us to be really ours, which it should be, but on the contrary seems the annihilation of our real existence. We try to encourage ourselves with secondary reflections that attempt to ennoble work in our eyes and to construct for it a kind of hagiographic legend,* but deep down inside of us there is something irrepressible always functioning, which never abandons protest and which

---

*The consecration of work, its positive interpretation, was one of the great new themes characteristic of the Renaissance, on which even the greatest antagonists—for example, Saint Ignatius of Loyola and Luther—are agreed. Work has been the "modern" virtue *par excellence*, the bourgeois virtue.

confirms the terrible curse of Genesis.* Hence the bad feeling we usually inject into the term "occupation." When someone tells us that he is "very occupied" he is usually giving us to understand that his real life is being held in suspension, as if foreign realities had invaded his world and left him without a home. This is true to such an extent that the man who works does so with the more or less vague hope of one day winning through work the liberation of his life, of being able in time to stop working and...to start really living.

All this indicates that man, painfully submerged in his work or obligatory occupations, projects beyond them, imagines another kind of life consisting of very different occupations, in the execution of which he would not feel as if he were losing time, but, on the contrary, gaining it, filling it satisfactorily and as it should be filled. Opposite a life which annihilates itself and fails—a life of work—he erects the plan of a life successful in itself—a life of delight and happiness. While obligatory occupations seem like foreign impositions, to those others we feel ourselves called by an intimate little voice that proclaims them from the innermost secret folds of our depths. This most strange phenomenon whereby we call on ourselves to do specific things is the "vocation."

There is one general vocation common to all men. All men, in fact, feel called on to be happy, but in each individual that general call becomes concrete in the more or less singular profile in which happiness appears to him. Happiness is a life dedicated to occupations for which that individual feels a singular vocation. Immersed in them, he misses nothing; the whole present fills him completely, free from desire and nostalgia. Laborious activities are performed, not out of any esteem for them, but rather for the result that follows them, but we give ourselves to vocational occupations for the pleasure of them, without concern for the subsequent profit. For that reason we want them never to end. We would like to eternalize, to perennialize them. And, really, once absorbed in a pleasurable occupation, we catch a starry glimpse of eternity.

So here is the human being suspended between two conflicting repertories of occupations: the laborious and the pleasing. It is moving and very sad to see how the two struggle in each individual. Work robs us of

---

*"In the sweat of thy face shalt thou eat bread" (Genesis 3:19).—Trans.

time to be happy, and pleasure gnaws away as much as possible at the time claimed by work. As soon as man discovers a chink or crack in the mesh of his work he escapes through it to the exercise of more enjoyable activities.

At this point a specific question, endowed with all the quasi-feminine appeal with which important questions are usually endowed, demands our attention. What kind of happy existence has man tried to attain when circumstances allowed him to do so? What have been the forms of the happy life? Even supposing that there have been many, innumerable, forms, have not some been clearly predominant? This is of the greatest importance, because in the happy occupations, again, the vocation of man is revealed. Nevertheless, we notice, surprised and scandalized, that this topic has never been investigated. Although it seems incredible, we lack completely a history of man's concept of what constitutes happiness.

Exceptional vocations aside, we confront the stupefying fact that, while obligatory occupations have undergone the most radical changes, the idea of the happy life has hardly varied throughout human evolution. In all times and places, as soon as man has enjoyed a moment's respite from his work, he has hastened, with illusion and excitement, to execute a limited and always similar repertory of enjoyable activities. Strange though this is, it is essentially true. To convince oneself, it is enough to proceed rather methodically, beginning by setting out the information.

What kind of man has been the least oppressed by work and the most easily able to engage in being happy? Obviously, the aristocratic man. Certainly the aristocrats too had their jobs, frequently the hardest of all: war, responsibilities of government, care of their own wealth. Only degenerate aristocracies stopped working, and complete idleness was short-lived because the degenerate aristocracies were soon swept away. But the work of the aristocrat, which looks more like "effort," was of such a nature that it left him a great deal of free time. And this is what concerns us: what does man do when, and in the extent that, he is free to do what he pleases? Now this greatly liberated man, the aristocrat, has always done the same things: raced horses or competed in physical exercises, gathered at parties, the feature of which is usually dancing, and engaged in conversation. But before any of those, and consistently more important than all of them has been...hunting. So that, if instead of speaking hypothetically we attend to the facts, we discover—whether we want to or not, with enjoyment or with anger—that the most appreciated, enjoyable occupation for the normal man has always been hunting. This is what kings and nobles have preferred to do: they have hunted. But it happens that the other social classes have done or wanted to do the same thing, to such an extent that one could almost divide the felicitous occupations of the normal man into four categories: hunting, dancing, racing, and conversing.

Choose at random any period in the vast and continuous flow of history and you will find that both men of the middle class and poor men have usually made hunting their happiest occupation. No one better represents the intermediary group between the Spanish nobility and Spanish bourgeoisie of the second half of the sixteenth century, than the Knight in the Green Overcoat, whom Don Quixote meets. In the plan of his life which he formally expounds, this knight makes clear that "his exercises are hunting and fishing." A man already in his fifties, he has given up the hound and the falcon; a partridge decoy and a bold ferret are enough for him. This is the least glorious kind of hunting, and it is understandable that Don Quixote shortly afterward, in a gesture of impatience that distorted his usual courtesy, scorned both beasts in comparison with the husky Moroccan lion, provided there by fortune for the voracity of his heroism.*

One of the few texts on the art of hunting which has come down to us from antiquity is the *Cynegeticus*, by Flavius Arrianus,** the historian of Alexander the Great, a Greek who wrote during the time of Antonius Pius and Marcus Aurelius. In this book, written during the first years of the second century A.D., Arrianus describes the hunting expeditions of the Celts and in unexpected detail studies separately the potentate's way of hunting, the middle-class man's way, and the lower-class way. That is, everybody hunted—out of pleasure, it is understood—in a civilization that corresponds roughly to the first Iron Age.

Nevertheless, the strongest proof of the extension throughout history of the enthusiasm for hunting lies in the contrary fact—namely, that with

---

* "Go, your grace, señor hidalgo, with your decoy partridge and your bold ferret, and let each one of us do his job" (Cervantes, *Don Quixote*, part II, chapter XVII).

** The author of the *Anabasis of Alexander*.—Trans.

maximum frequency throughout the centuries not everyone has been allowed to hunt. A privilege has been made of this occupation, one of the most characteristic privileges of the powerful. Precisely because almost all men wanted to hunt and saw a possible happiness in doing so, it was necessary to stagger the exercise of the occupation; otherwise the game would have very soon disappeared, and neither the many nor the few would have been happy in that situation. It is not improbable, then, that even in the Neolithic period hunting acquired some of the aspects of a privilege. Neolithic man, who is already cultivating the soil, who has tamed animals and breeds them, does not need, as did his Paleolithic predecessor, to feed himself principally from his hunting. Freed of its obligatory nature, hunting is elevated to the rank of a sport. Neolithic man is already rich, and this means that he lives in authentic societies; thus in societies divided into classes, with their inevitable "upper" and "lower." It is difficult to imagine that hunting was not limited in one way or another.

Once we have underlined the almost universally privileged nature of the sport of hunting, it becomes clear to what extent this is no laughing matter but rather, however strangely, a deep and permanent yearning in the human condition. It is as if we had poked a trigeminal nerve. From all the revolutionary periods in history, there leaps into view the lower classes' fierce hatred for the upper classes because the latter had limited hunting—an indication of the enormous appetite which the lower classes had for the occupation. One of the causes of the French Revolution was the irritation the country people felt because they were not allowed to hunt, and consequently one of the first privileges which the nobles were obliged to abandon was this one. In all revolutions, the first thing that the "people" have done was to jump over the fences of the preserves or to tear them down, and in the name of social justice pursue the hare and the partridge. And this after the revolutionary newspapers, in their editorials, had for years and years been abusing the aristocrats for being so frivolous as to...spend their time hunting.

About 1938, Jules Romains, a hardened writer of the Front Populaire, published an article venting his irritation with the workers, because they, having gained a tremendous reduction in the work day and being in possession of long idle hours, had not learned to occupy themselves other than in the most uncouth form of hunting: fishing with a rod, the favorite sport of the good French bourgeois. The ill-humored writer was deeply irritated that a serious revolution had been achieved with no apparent result other than that of augmenting the number of rod fishermen.

The chronic fury of the people against the privilege of hunting is not, then, incidental or mere subversive insolence. It is thoroughly justified: in it the people reveal that they are men like those of the upper class and that the vocation, the felicitous illusion, of hunting, is normal in the human being. What is an error is to believe that this privilege has an arbitrary origin, that it is pure injustice and abuse of power. No; we shall presently see why hunting—not only the luxurious sporting variety, but any and all forms of hunting—essentially demands limitation and privilege.

Argue, fight as much as you like, over who should be the privileged ones, but do not pretend that squares are round and that hunting is not a privilege. What happens here is just what has happened with many other things. For two hundred years Western man has been fighting to eliminate privilege, which is stupid, because in certain orders privilege is inevitable and its existence does not depend on human will. It is to be hoped that the West will dedicate the next two centuries to fighting—here is no hope for a suspension of its innate pugnacity—to fighting, I say, for something less stupid, more attainable, and not at all extraordinary, such as a better selection of privileged persons.

In periods of an opposite nature, which were not revolutionary and in which, avoiding false utopias, people relied on things as they really were, not only was hunting a privilege respected by all, but those on the bottom demanded it of those on top, because they saw in hunting, especially in its superior forms—the chase, falconry, and the battue*—a vigorous discipline and an opportunity to show courage, endurance, and skill, which are the attributes of the genuinely powerful person. Once a crown prince who had grown up in Rome went to occupy the Persian throne. Very soon he had to abdicate because the Persians could not accept a monarch who did not like hunting, a traditional and almost titular occupation of Persian gentlemen. The young man, apparently, had become interested in literature and was beyond hope.

---

* Practice of beating woods to drive the game from cover.—Trans.

Hunting, like all human occupations, has its different levels, and how little of the real work of hunting is suggested in words like diversion, relaxation, entertainment! A good hunter's way of hunting is a hard job which demands much from man: he must keep himself fit, face extreme fatigues, accept danger. It involves a complete code of ethics of the most distinguished design; the hunter who accepts the sporting code of ethics keeps his commandments in the greatest solitude, with no witnesses or audience other than the sharp peaks of the mountain, the roaming cloud, the stern oak, the trembling juniper, and the passing animal. In this way hunting resembles the monastic rule and the military order. So, in my presentation of it as what it is, as a form of happiness, I have avoided calling it pleasure. Doubtless in all happiness there is pleasure, but pleasure is the least of happiness. Pleasure is a passive occurrence, and it is appropriate to return to Aristotle, for whom happiness always clearly consisted in an act, in an energetic effort. That this effort, as it is being performed, produces pleasure is only coincidental, and, if you wish, one of the ingredients that comprise the situation. But along with the pleasures which exist in hunting, there are innumerable annoyances. What right have we to take it by that handle and not by this one? The truth is that the important and appealing aspect of hunting is neither pleasure nor annoyance, but rather the very activity that comprises hunting.

Happy occupations, it is clear, are not merely pleasures; they are efforts, and real sports are effort. It is not possible, then, to distinguish work from sport by a plus or minus in fatigue. The difference is that sport is an effort made completely freely, for the pure enjoyment of it, while work is an obligatory effort made with an eye to the profit.*

---

* This is the "living" counterposition in the original meaning of the word "sport"— that is, in its etymology. (Etymologies are not merely of linguistic interest, they also enable us to discover situations really "lived" by man which remain preserved *with the full freshness of present time*, like the flesh of the mammoths preserved for millennia in the Siberian ice, which has been eaten by present-day men.) The word "sport" has entered the common language from the guild-hall language of Mediterranean sailors whose hard life at sea stood opposite their pleasurable life in port. "Sport" (in Spanish *deporte*) is "to be in port" (*de portu*). But port life is not only the sailor planted on the dock, with his

hands in his trouser pockets and his pipe between his teeth, staring obsessively at the horizon as if he expected islands to blossom on its liquid line. There are, first of all, the interminable discussions in the port taverns between sailors of the most diverse nations. These conversations have been one of the most efficient organs of civilization. In them different and distant cultures have been transmitted and have clashed. There are also the sporting games of strength and skill. The word appears to have already been accepted in the troubadour culture of Provence, and frequently in the combination *deports* and *solatz* (sport and solace), where, in contrast with modern use, sport was rather the game of conversation and poetry, while solace represented the physical exercises: hunting, lances, jousts, rings, and dances. In the offficial chronicle for Henry IV [King of Castile and Leon 1454–1474], the verb 'to *sport*' is used in reference to hunting [Alfonso de Palencia, *Crónica de Enrique IV* (Madrid: *Revista de Archivos*, 1904–1909)]. Today we would judge this image a Gallicism and so it was then—it was a Provence-ism. It is well to remember that Gallicisms are not an invention of these last decades.

[The similar English words "disport" and its abbreviation "sport" do not appear to be derived from "port" in the sense of harbor; however, the definitions of both those words include the idea of "diversion."—Trans.]

Polybius
and
Scipio Æmilianus

These inherent qualities of effort and exploit which comprise hunting at its best have meant that it has always been considered a great education, one of the preferred methods of training character. Only in the contemporary period and, within that, only in the most demoralized regions of Europe has an affinity for hunting been held in disesteem.

Against this background, it is an opportune moment for me to point out a remarkable exemplar, which, although I do not understand why, no one has properly emphasized until now. It may not excite the reader. It does me, profoundly, and with me all those capable of feeling under their feet the pulsation of the profound human past, of which, like it or not, we are no more than the present and superficial emergence. I refer to the fact that one of the most illustrious friendships ever to have existed on the planet earth—the friendship between the Greek historian Polybius and the Roman aristocrat Scipio Æmilianus (Scipio Africanus the Younger)—was occasioned by and based on their common interest in hunting.

I do not cite this exemplar as a matter of academic sanctimony. After having coined the term "sanctimony of culture," I have pursued the thing itself without pause wherever it is found. For almost forty years, throughout my existence, I have put myself out, day after day, to push my compatriots and the entire Spanish-speaking world toward a culture without sanctimony, in which everything might be lively and authentic, the estimable esteemed and the fallacious eliminated. But people will have to stop being beasts and manage to tremble when it is time to tremble, which is not only at the moment of death, but whenever there is in sight

some symptom of superior humanity. Anything else is rusticity and stupidity.

Polybius and Scipio Æmilianus represent two authentic peaks of man-
hood, not two worthless scholarly names cited to show off my erudition.

Polybius (205?–?125 B.C.) was one of the few great minds which the
turbid human species has managed to produce. Born when the destiny
of Greece was declining, he sums up in his single person the whole trea-
sure of vital experiences, of intellectual and political order, of personal
and collective bias which the Hellenic world had forged. A statesman, a
soldier, an engineer, he is one of the few "classical" men free of rhetoric.
He is a man of things, in the principal meaning that this word (Latin, *res*;
Greek, *pragmata*) had for Romans and Greeks; that is to say, that he is a
man of "affairs." Consequently he is concerned only with what he calls
"pragmatic thought"—that is, technical thought—and he calls his way of
writing history "pragmatic history." The historic fact did not interest him
because of its factual nature, much less as a pretext, as it was for many of
the ancient historians, to compose, while narrating it, a compact tragedy
that would excite the readers' viscera. He was interested in the "why" of
the fact; his *History* is a clear precursory example of what I have called
"historic reason." And even this reason has a technical preference: technique of arms, tactics, or strategy, techniques of institutions or geogra-
phy; in short, the specific technique of history itself. He composed the
first universal history, giving to this concept such a rigorous and penetrating meaning that we have not yet surpassed his understanding. For the
present, however, what is important is the fact that in his lifetime the
western and eastern civilizations of the Mediterranean, which together
made up the inhabited part of the earth, had come to join and converge.
He wrote, then, a universal history because he realized that the living
human reality had become universal. His country, Megalopolis, sent him
to Rome, first as a hostage, and later, in view of the influence he acquired
there, as an ambassador. For his historic investigations, not trusting anybody, he traversed almost all the countries known at the time, to see
things with his own eyes and to hear the information pour forth from the
original sources. A tireless traveler, he died at the age of eighty as is a
traveler's due, falling off his horse. This is one of the men.

The other is Scipio Æmilianus (185–129 B.C.) He is the culminating figure of ascendant Roman history; after him the decline begins. He foresees it clearly and this adds to his profile a quivering edge of fatal melancholy. He is, then, at the divide of Roman destinies: rise and fall, integration and disintegration. In him the energetic and ascetic virtues that forged the power of Rome reach their extreme maturity. But he is also the first Roman leader to assimilate the Hellenic culture; his house the first among the consulate houses where Greek is spoken, and he himself the first Roman citizen to shave every day. Consequently, in his person which contains the best of the Latin past there now appears the Roman future, and if we look at his soul against the light we catch a glimpse of the remote silhouettes of Caesar, Augustus, and Trajan. But Scipio is still the completely normal Roman; he is the superlative of Roman sanity. Later perhaps there will be another man with greater genius—Caesar, for example. But Caesar, besides being a genius, is already a monster. In reality, after Scipio Æmilianus, Rome produced hardly anything but monsters. Through the veins of this Scipio flows a mixture of two of the oldest and most exquisite "bloods" of Rome: that of the *gens* Æmilianus, that of the *gens* Cornelius. The Scipios are Cornelians. Scipio the Great, the first Scipio Africanus, was our Scipio's adoptive grandfather and his blood relative on his mother's side. But the Scipios also belong to Spain. They conquered the Spanish in the double meaning of that word: they conquered them and they convinced them, they tamed them and they inspired them. According to the Roman juridical institution, the Spaniards were clients of the Scipios. They protected them in the face of the Roman senate. This also obliged them to make crude interventions in Spain. Scipio Æmilianus besieged and destroyed Numantia. Near him in camp was Polybius, a technician of strategy and an engineer, inventor of siege engines, perfecter of the military signal system, of what is today called "transmission." We Spaniards do not bear a grudge because of the bold action that these men took against our ancestors. Without it, and other similar actions, the soul of the peninsular Spaniard would not have that hard foundation of Roman masonry which is always present in the Spaniard, and which, however much time advances, perennially makes him an "ancient man." Roman discipline, brought to the peninsula by the Scipios, domesticated the Spaniards of that time, who, like those of today, were as brave as they were frenetic. Scipio Æmilianus was chaste at a time when, according to Polybius, the victory over Perseus of Macedonia had infected the Romans with sensuality and made them discover homosexuality. Scipio Æmilianus was impartial and generous. "Such generosity," Polybius also tells us, "deserves admiration everywhere, but especially in Rome, where no one willingly gives up what is his." Polybius's text demands a scrupulous commentary, because one of the secrets of why Rome became Rome becomes apparent in it. Scipio Æmilianus was a great general. He restored the gravely demoralized Roman army.* He was serious and kind. He neither sought power nor turned away from it. He was assassinated, of course. This is the other man.

And between one man and the other, so different in nationality and age, there began an indestructible friendship. When they met, Polybius was thirty-four years old and Scipio eighteen. When Polybius reaches the point in his *History*** of recounting the victory of Paulus Æmilius, Scipio's natural father, over Perseus, the last king of Macedonia, he thinks it appropriate to suspend his narration of the great events to let slip one of the very few bits of intimate memories which antiquity has left us. Perhaps the most radical difference between the man of antiquity and the one who succeeded him in the West—that is to say, us—lies in the fact that ancient man was strangely lacking in intimacy. Polybius's work is, then, an exceptional text in many ways, and it is appropriate to reproduce here his pertinent passages about hunting, since it is one of the culminating facts in the universal history of man the hunter.

> *And since the opportunity to speak of this illustrious family presents itself, I will keep the promise made in the first book to say when, how, and why Scipio acquired in Rome a reputation beyond his years, and how our friendship became so intimate, to the point of being known not only in Italy and Greece, but also in the more distant countries.*

---

* The need to do this was what caused him to commit that atrocity at Numantia.
** Only a quarter of the *History* survives; this is, without question, one of the gravest losses that we have suffered in our Greco-Roman heritage.

I have already said that our relationship began with conversations about the books that he loaned me...

After reproducing some of their first talks and describing at length Scipio's virtues he adds:

He needed to distinguish himself for his strength and valor, qualities which are esteemed above all others in almost all nations, but especially in Rome. To do so he needed to train himself a great deal, and Fortune provided him with a propitious opportunity. The kings of Macedonia were exceedingly fond of hunting *and had large parks full of beasts. During the war, preoccupied with things of greater importance, Perseus did not bother to hunt, and in those four years the game multiplied extraordinarily. When the war was over, and Paulus Aemilius was convinced that that was the most useful and noble diversion for his sons, he gave Scipio the servants that the king had for that sport and the liberty to hunt as much as he wanted. Considering himself almost a king, the young man busied himself with nothing else the whole time that the legions remained in Macedonia after the battle and took advantage of the liberty granted him all the more because, having the vigor of youth,* he was naturally a fan of this sport, *and like a noble greyhound, indefatigable in engaging in it. Back again in Rome,* he found in me the same passion for hunting *and this made his own increase; so while other young Romans used their time pleading lawsuits, flattering judges, or visiting the Forum, trying to acquire fame by means of such occupations,* Scipio, *dedicated to hunting, was acquiring a better reputation than they with his daring undertakings of this sort; because an undertaking in the Forum always injures some citizen, the one who loses the case, while the enterprise undertaken by Scipio, since he aspires to be among the best, not by speeches but by deeds, does not hurt anyone. The truth is that in a short time he surpassed in reputation all Romans of his own age, no one having been more highly esteemed, although to get there he took a different route from the one usually followed in Rome.*

Polybius and Scipio Æmilianus were, then, passionate hunters. Enough said.

The Essence
of Hunting

ow that we have fully realized that hunting is such a universal and impassioned sport—that is, that it belongs in the repertory of the purest forms of human happiness—the realization only serves to increase even more our appetite for inquiring, for observing, even if from far away, why this is so. But this cannot be ascertained if we do not first ascertain what hunting is. What is the nature of the venatic act which, apparently, has always had the ability to rouse men's enthusiasm? We are not now interested, therefore, in this or that *which has to do with hunting*, what refers to it and what applies to it, but rather in what hunting itself is or, as we should say, the *essence* of hunting.

So let us work toward a definition of hunting. Everything that does not do this is a digression, and we must never be content with mere ornaments and pretty penmanship.

That hunting is a sport is incidental. There is also the purely utilitarian form of hunting, which was practiced by Paleolithic man and which the poacher of any epoch practices. This type of hunting, not at all sporting, is no less hunting than is the other type.

Hunting cannot be defined by its transient purposes—utilitarian or sporting. They remain outside of it, beyond it, and they presuppose it. We hunt to divert ourselves or to feed ourselves, but these ends to which we freely apply hunting imply that hunting already *is*, and that it has its own consistency before, or apart from, those ends. The different ends attributed to hunting do not essentially determine the operation which is its substance, but rather, as we shall see, they modulate only its exercise, they stylize it. There is the style of the sporting hunter and there is the style of the professional hunter, on which I will comment later.

Nor can hunting be defined by its particular operations, its techniques. These are innumerable, very diverse, and no one can pretend to be the essence of hunting. Each and every one implies certain general and common assumptions which are the true essence of hunting. Therefore it is an error to define hunting, as does Kurt Lindner in his book *Prehistoric Hunting*,* as a "reasoned pursuit." First of all, who can say what constituted reason in *Homo Heidelbergensis* or in his friend from Altamira! It is more than clear that these men, or "hominoids," the most ancient that we have glimpsed, did not invent hunting but rather received it from their prehuman past, free from that which people call reason and to which they so glibly refer, as if it were a very clear matter. Paleolithic man already used traps and nets to capture the animal, but it seems that the spider spins his prodigious web for a predatory purpose, as does the ferocious ant lion build his conical hole, which made Renan's hair stand on end. But there is also this fact, the substance of which will be seen at the end of the present analysis: a task in which rational intervention is the decisive factor, becomes, for the same reason, susceptible to great, continuous progress—in principle, unlimited progress. Now, it is characteristic of hunting to have hardly changed in its general structure since ancient times. The marvelous scene of a deer hunt in the Cueva de los Caballos [Cave of Horses] in the Castellón province of Valencia, which dates from the Paleolithic Age, does not differ in any important way from a photograph of a hunting party out by Valdegrana or Mezquetillas. The only difference is in the weapon, which then was the bow and arrow, while now it is the rifle. But changes that have to do with weapons—that is to say with a greater effectiveness in the actual killing of the animal—do not count as essential changes, because if we did not get off on the wrong foot at the beginning of this meditation we will realize now that killing is not the *exclusive* purpose of hunting. There are kinds of hunting that consist in "bringing the animal back alive," and the early men who domesticated animals tried to take them without killing them.**

---

* Kurt Lindner, *La chasse préhistorique* (Paris: Payot, 1941).
** I discuss later the practice of contenting oneself with photographing the animal.

Furthermore, if I anticipate something which the reader will only later be able to see with complete clarity, I will prove, as effectively as would evidence, that progress in weapons is foreign to the essence of hunting, that reason is not a primary ingredient of it, since *hunting cannot substantially progress*. This is so true that hardly had the weapon been perfected when all urgency for putting an end to the animal, by whatever means, disappeared—that is to say, hunting became a sport. And since then, *as the weapon became more and more effective, man imposed more and more limitations on himself as the animal's rival in order to leave it free to practice its wily defenses, in order to avoid making the prey and the hunter excessively unequal, as if passing beyond a certain limit in that relationship might annihilate the essential character of the hunt, transforming it into pure killing and destruction.* Hence the confrontation between man and animal has a precise boundary beyond which hunting ceases to be hunting, just at the point where man lets loose his immense technical superiority—that is, rational superiority—over the animal. The fisherman who poisons the mountain brook to annihilate suddenly, all at once, the trout swimming in it, *ipso facto* ceases to be a hunter. The same is true of the man who uses excessively effective means to rid the mountains of rabbits or beatifically kills flies and ants by spraying the atmosphere or the house with Flit. To exterminate or to destroy animals by an invincible and automatic procedure is not hunting.* Hunting is something else, something more delicate.

Nothing stands in the way of our discovering what hunting is as much as does this inopportune rush to involve reason in the definition. Soon we shall see that in present-day hunting—and it has always been more or less like this—reason's most important intervention consists precisely in its restraining itself, in its limiting its own intervention. Thanks to this restraint hunting subsists; so, far from hunting's being a "reasoned pursuit," reason can be described more appropriately as the greatest danger to the existence of hunting.

These difficulties in defining the act of hunting originate in the fact that those concerned with this topic, distrustful of their own conceptual

---

* Let me be absolutely clear: I do not mean that doing this would not be hunting for sport. No, no; the fact is that it would not be hunting at all!

agility, are afraid of confusing the issue even more if they accept the most obvious thing in the world—namely, that hunting is not an exclusively human occupation, but occurs throughout almost the entire zoological scale. Only a definition of hunting that is based on the complete extension of this immense fact, and covering equally the beast's predatory zeal and any good hunter's almost mystical agitation, will get to the root of this surprising phenomenon. Anything else will leave it up in the air, or, as we say in Castile, would be to grab the radish by the leaves.

The cat hunts rats. The lion hunts antelopes. The sphex and other wasps hunt caterpillars and grubs. The spider hunts flies. The shark hunts smaller fish. The bird of prey hunts rabbits and doves. Thus, hunting goes on throughout almost all of the animal kingdom. There is hardly a class or phylum in which groups of hunting animals do not appear. Hunting is, therefore, not even peculiar to mammals.

If we take a look at the features common to the many different forms of hunting we come up for the time being with the fact that hunting is an occurrence between two animals, one of which is the agent and the other the subject, one the hunter and the other the hunted. If the hunted is also, on the same occasion, a hunter, this is not hunting; it is combat, a fight in which both parties have the same intention and similar behavior. Fighting is a reciprocal action. The gladiator in the arena did not hunt the panther that had been let out of the cage; he fought with it, because neither found himself in a natural situation. In the course of hunting a fight may occur, as in the case of the wild boar which, when cornered, turns and attacks the hunter; but this fight has only incidental significance within the hunt, and whatever grave consequences may result, it is only an anecdote embroidered on the main tapestry of hunting. If the hunted animal were normally to fight with man, so that the relationship between the two consisted in this fight, we would have a completely different phenomenon. For this reason, bullfighting is not hunting. Neither does the man hunt the bull, nor does the bull, upon attacking, do so with hunting intentions the bullfight is, in effect, *something like* a fight but so *sui generis* that, strictly speaking, it is not that either.

Fighting is mutual aggression. In hunting, however, the question is always that of one animal striving to hunt, while the other strives to not be hunted. Hunting is not reciprocal. And the reason it is not is because it is a relationship between animals *which excludes an equality of vital level between the two*, and, of course, it excludes even more the possibility of an inferior animal's practicing it on a superior animal. The lion, when it comes across a tiger, does not try to hunt it; rather, he either lets it pass, or he fights it, because he knows that the tiger is going to do the same with him. Their near equality is so famous that the preferred topic of discussion in provincial clubs is whether the lion or the tiger is the king of the veld.*

The essential inequality between the prey and the hunter does not keep the pursued animal from being able to surpass the pursuer in one endowment or another: he may be faster or stronger or more perceptive. However, in the general balance of vital endowments, the hunter will always have the advantage over the hunted. Hunting is irremediably an activity from above to below

Thus, without our seeking it, the universal fact of hunting reveals to us the inequality of level among the species—the zoological hierarchy.

Instead of seeking the definition of hunting in its techniques or in the transient ends to which we apply it, we must extract it from the inherent goal which becomes apparent in the activity of the hunter. This inherent goal is simply its final stage, its conclusion when the activity is completed—that is to say, when the hunting expedition is successful. Then the hunt ends simply in the hunter's taking possession of the prey, dead or alive.** This is why, leaving aside the reciprocity of pursuit in the bullfight, I said earlier that neither does the bullfighter hunt the bull nor does the bull hunt the bullfighter, despite the fact that both go for the body and do not beat around the bush. But neither the bullfighter nor the bull seeks "to take possession" of the other. The bull attacks with an intention almost exactly opposite to that of "taking possession." The bull does not want *to have* the bull fighter dead or alive; on the contrary, he wants to

---

* Ortega has chosen a highly hypothetical example; nowadays, the lion, an animal of open plains, is found only in Africa, except for a few examples in southwest Asia; the tiger, a forest animal, only in Asia.—Trans.

** Thus Plato in the *Euthydemus* (290, B): "Hunting is nothing more than pursuing the game and laying hands on it; as to what is done with that on which one has laid one's hands, once one has laid one's hands on it, this is not pertinent to the hunt." [This footnote, found among the unedited papers of the author, was added by the editors at Revista de Occidente. S.A., Madrid, 1960.]

eliminate him, to annihilate him, to "get him out of his sight," to make him disappear. So when he has gored him as much as he wants and has the impression that he no longer exists, he leaves the fighter there; he abandons him and simply proceeds to other business.* In contrast, the acts involved in hunting are all shaped by the purpose and end of *having* the prey, or "retrieving it."

At this point we are sufficiently prepared for a definition, the implications and corollaries of which will follow.

Hunting is what an animal does to take possession, dead or alive, of some other being that belongs to a species basically inferior to its own. Vice versa, if there is to be a hunt, this superiority of the hunter over the prey *cannot be absolute*. Here is where the matter begins to be really subtle and interesting.

Do not forget that we are talking now not only about hunting as a sport, but rather about all kinds of hunting, the human variety as well as the subhuman. Well, then, for this precise event that we call hunting really to happen, it is necessary that the hunted animal have his chance, that he be able, in principle, to avoid capture; that is to say, that he possess means of some degree of effectiveness to escape from the pursuit, because hunting is precisely the series of efforts and skills which the hunter has to exercise to dominate with sufficient frequency the countermeasures of the animal which is the object of the hunt. If these countermeasures did not exist, if the inferiority of the animal were absolute, the opportunity to put the activities involved in hunting into effect would not have occurred, or, to say it another way, the peculiar fact of the hunt would not exist. When I contrast the hunted to the hunter, I mean the sought and pursued, which may very well not be the possessed. *It is not essential to the hunt that it be successful.* On the contrary, if the hunter's efforts were always and inevitably successful it would not be the effort we call hunting, it would be something else. Corresponding to the even-

---

* As far as what the bullfighter intends to do with the bull is concerned, this cannot be explained in a few words, because it is a very subtle matter. Naturally he does not have the same intention toward the bull that the bull has toward him. What interests him is not the elimination of the bull by killing it. This kind of killing, its meaning and existence, is a secret in the history of bullfighting which I am not going to look into here.

tuality or chance of the prey's escaping is the eventuality of the hunter's *rentrer bredouille* [going home emptyhanded].* The beauty of hunting lies in the fact that it is always problematic.

The hunting species and the hunted species, therefore, have to find themselves a very specific distance apart on the zoological scale. The venatic relationship cannot be provoked at less than nor more than that distance between them. As I have already said, one does not hunt a superior or an almost equal, but neither does one hunt the excessively inferior, because then the latter cannot use his wiles. The sportsman is in error if he thinks this arises from the pure gentlemanliness of a Knight of the Round Table, he who invented the idea of leaving the animal free to use its wiles. Doubtless, man opens this margin to the beast deliberately and of his own free will. He could annihilate quickly and easily most animal species, or at least precisely those that he delights in hunting. Far from doing that, he restrains his destructive power, limits and regulates it—the veto *par excellence* is the closed season; he strives to insure the life of the species, and, above all, in the venatic dealing with animals he leaves them, in effect, free to play their own "game." But in this he does nothing more than *imitate Nature*. Infrahuman hunting is in itself that "game," and anything else would not be hunting. If man wants to hunt, he can only, like it or not, make this concession to the animal. This is why I say that it is not pure gentlemanliness. If man did not do this he would not only destroy animals, he would also destroy, coincidentally, the very act of hunting which fascinates him. *There is, then, in the hunt as a sport a supremely free renunciation by man of the supremacy of his humanity.* Instead of doing all that he could do as man, he restrains his excessive endowments and begins to imitate Nature—that is, for pleasure he returns to Nature and re-enters it. Perhaps this is a first glimpse of why hunting is such a great delight for man. We will see later.

The hunting animal works at his predatory task motivated by an *ad hoc* set of definite instincts that his species possesses. For this reason each species has its own peculiar way of hunting, a way that hardly var-

---

* Does there exist in the pure vocabulary of the hunt any other phrase which says this with as much expression as the French phrase? It would be interesting to know.

ies. But in turn the species hunted by it rely on a set of defensive instincts that makes their capture difficult. This is what hunting really is: *a contest or confrontation between two systems of instincts.* But for this to occur it is necessary that those instincts—not only the hunter's, but also the prey's—function freely. This free functioning of the instincts on the part of the pursued animal is what I have called its "game." If this is eliminated, the typical zoological fact that we call hunting is eliminated too. In the "game" in which Nature on the one hand and man's sporting will on the other place it, the animal acts with sufficient ease so that his instinctive resources can complete their operation. This happens even in hunting which uses a trap or snare. The proof of it is that the trap or snare consists precisely in finding a way of fighting the prodigious instincts of suspiciousness always alert in the beast. The smallest disturbance of the countryside arouses him. The animal has the instinct that "there are traps set," surreptitious and disguised threats everywhere, the indication of which is the smallest abnormality around him. The hunt is not something which happens to the animal by chance; rather in the instinctive depths of his nature he has already foreseen the hunter. So that it is one of the great instruments which Nature uses to regulate life on the planet! *"Les espèces,"* said Cuvier, *"sont nécessaires, les unes commes proies, les autres comme destructeurs et modérateurs de propagation. On ne peut se représenter rationnellement un état de choses où il y aurait des mouches sans hirondelles et reciproquement."** The only things that escape the animal's sensibility are those which are not natural. In the high land of Ávila, in Campoazálvaro, an extraordinary and frightening Tibetan-like valley, I have been able to shoot grouse and ducks, very suspicious people, at very close range, thanks to the fact that I rolled along in an automobile through the stubble. Instinctively the animal fears man, who has been created by Nature, but he does not fear the unnatural artifact of human fabrication.

---

* "The different species are necessary, some as prey, others as destroyers and moderators of propagation. One cannot rationally imagine a state of things where there would be flies without swallows and vice versa" (Baron Georges Cuvier [1769–1832], French zoologist).—Trans.

It is terrible and wondrous to contemplate how each hunting species is associated with a group of species which are its prey.* The profile of the hunter's aggressive capacity fits exactly the profile of the hunted's defensive and evasive capacity. Which makes us realize that there is no universal hunter, an eminent confirmation of our thesis: that hunting implies an inequality among the species, but that this inequality cannot be excessive. *Aquila non capit muscas*.** Man is a good example even though he is the hunter with the broadest range of prey. Man does not hunt ants, and the term "microbe hunters" used in a very entertaining book is just a figure of speech. And notice that as the hunter becomes more refined, he eliminates species from his venatic orbit until he has very few left— namely, the ones which conserve more of their cunning game in the face of man. Some men hunt only big game, snubbing, for example, rabbit, hare, or partridge.

Each act concretely executed by the hunter is, then, a means provoked by a countermeasure of evasion which the prey possesses. These countermeasures are innumerable and many of them are extremely well known. But usually one thinks only of concrete acts of defense which, while the most obvious, are also the least effective: the ability to run fast, swift flight, a strong sense of smell, a watchful eye. One forgets that the entire life of the animal is shaped by the incessant wait for an aggression; for him living is being perpetually alert for the hunter, who sometimes does not exist. More than flying, running, and watching, the beast's nocturnal customs protect him. Here we have a biological mystery, the obvious and usual explanation for which does nothing more than increase the mystery. It is tragic that marvelous animals, which one need only contemplate to understand that they are made for daylight, have distorted their existence, making night out of day, and vice versa.

---

* See The Ethics of Hunting, pp. 97ff.
** The eagle does not hunt flies.—Trans.

The
Scarcity of
Game

ertain species, especially those most interesting to man, possess a countermeasure even less visible, to the degree that it consists precisely in invisibility. *This countermeasure, fundamental and prior to all others, is scarcity.* No one has ever remarked on the radical aspect of this point, which is its interesting aspect.

Anyone who is now advanced in years has had the opportunity to observe that, from his childhood to the present, the number of animals interesting to the human hunter has greatly diminished. To explain this, obvious reasons have been given: the greater perfection of weapons; the excessive number of hunters that use them; the growing area of cultivated lands not only in Europe but throughout the world. Whether or not these are the causes, the diminution itself is fact, and once reality has forced us to accept it as such, it triggers in us an abstract line of reasoning. If in our childhood there was more game than today, going backward in time we should find greater and greater abundance and we should presently arrive at times in which it must have been superabundant. This is how we have got into our heads, almost automatically, the common conviction that "Before, there was much more game," in the sense that "There was more than enough game." I myself have accepted this like everyone else.

This is a good example of what I have called "inertial thinking," in that the mind, under the impulse of an observation or idea true in itself, continues thinking vaguely and mechanically in the same direction.* On

* The most illustrious example of "inertial thinking" is arithmetic. Once we have learned that a number is formed by adding one unit to another we continue adding units and forming numbers to infinity. This is done mechanically and requires no perspicacity at all: This why Hegel calls mathematics *entäussertes Denken*—extrinsic, alienated

the other hand, "alert thought" is always ready to rectify its trajectory, to break its direction, attentive to the reality outside it.

Many years ago, reading an account of the reign of John II in the *Chronicles of the Kings of Castile,** I came upon these lines:

> *On Friday the 28th of November of this same year (1449), the Prince left Toledo to go hunting in the thicket at Requena, which belongs to the monks of the Huelgas of Burgos, to kill a great boar which he had been told was to be found in the same thicket; and he sent for more than one thousand persons to come from Ocaña and Yepes and that region to surround the thicket. And as the Prince entered the thicket and the boar found itself surrounded, it jumped into the Tajo [Tagus] River, which is near the thicket, and it swam across, so that no one, neither on foot, nor on horseback, dared to prevent it from crossing the river; and for pleasure the Prince spent four days hunting in that thicket*

Reading this I was stupefied. What—in the middle of the fifteenth century, when no weapon other than the javelin or the lance** was used in big-game hunting, the appearance of a wild boar in the great solitude of a Toledan thicket was such an extraordinary thing that the opportunity to enjoy the delights of hunting it was reason enough to detain a king? Certainly, it must have been an unusually big animal, but, since a certain proportion exists between the number of animals and the number of gigantic ones, the almost warlike mobilization of the game beaters reveals how unusual the incident was. But can it be that game was scarce

thought, in which the spirit does not need to be present while operating. Remember that inertia does not mean quietude but rather perseverance in a state, whatever it may be, whether repose or movement. This "inertial thinking" is the opposite of "alert thought," and therefore Hegel humorously makes it clear than when we suffer insomnia a good remedy is to count, which reveals that counting is not a task that demands vivacity. Keep this in mind for the section entitled The Hunter—the Alert Man (pp. 137-140).

    * This title is incorrectly cited by Ortega. The quotation which follows actually comes from Fernán Pérez de Guzmán, *Crónica del señor rey Don Juan, segundo de este nombre en Castilla y Leon*...[Chronicle of His Majesty, King John, second of this name in Castile and Leon...], edited by Lorenzo Galindez de Carvajal (Valencia, 1779), chapter IX, p. 544.—Trans.

    ** The Moorish long musket, rough and heavy, still appeared here and there, but I doubt that it was still used in hunting.

in the European Middle Ages too? The incident itself was not important to me, but it became an obsession because the information produced a traumatic "shock" in a conviction, however insignificant, that I, inertially, had thought very firm. It was a sign that one must live in a perpetual state of detachment before one's own convictions. It could very easily have been a chronicler's mistake, and perhaps the reading of those lines had astonished his contemporaries too; by contradicting a well-known fact: the abundance of game. But no such thing.

Once on the track, we find everywhere substantial proof that game animals have always been scarce. In *Amadís de Gaula* [Amadis of Gaul], which was written a few years after that chronicle, or maybe around the same date, chapter XXIII of the first book begins like this:

> *Since King Lisuarte was very fond of hunting, when he was free from other things that were more important to his position, he often went hunting in the woods which were near Vindilisora,* because, since they were very closely guarded, *there were many wild animals and also deer there.*

This is not a matter of an isolated statement that can be attributed to insufficient information. Here the author, who wrote for the aristocrats of his time, takes for granted that only on an exceptionally well-guarded estate could the game not be scarce. Furthermore the *Amadís* is not a realistic book; rather, everything in it is portrayed as perfect, polished, and idealized to the point of saturation. So, even in imaginary Vindilisora —which is simply a fantasy Windsor—the abundance of deer has to be taken with a grain of salt. So much for the Middle Ages.

But in the earlier quotation from Polybius we came across the same thing in reference to the second century before Christ, in one of the wildest regions of the continent, Macedonia. The only difference is that there it is stated more precisely. The abundance of game in any spot was evidently such an unusual phenomenon that Polybius thinks he must explain it in this particular case. The fact that the parks are carefully guarded is not enough, apparently, to account for the abundance of game; the abnormal circumstance that the owner, Perseus, did not hunt for four years is also necessary. This is what Polybius says, but without his intending them to, his words reveal more. If he considers this park's being opened to Scipio "a propitious occasion provided by Fortune," then a young Roman aristocrat—during the time that Rome was the most powerful nation in the world—did not find such an opportunity to hunt a common occurrence.*

The validity of these two texts applies throughout both periods: ancient times and the Middle Ages. They are, furthermore, so representative that we need not mention innumerable others, because they would not supply us with more information.** If we add to this our modern experience we can say with complete certainty that in all known history game has never abounded.

But before history come the vast millennia of prehistory, and in them the Paleolithic Age, the time in which man was occupied solely in hunting.

Prehistorians usually affirm that the various glacial and postglacial periods were paradise for the hunter. They give us the impression that tasty prey swarmed everywhere in unimaginable abundance, and reading their works, the wild animal that dozes deep down inside any good hunter feels his teeth sharpen and his mouth water. But those appraisals are vague and summary. At times, a precise bit of information, in which we are given figures, leads us to imagine swarms of animals. Thus, the

---

* It is clear that, as always, Polybius knows what he is talking about. There is a detail in the text that makes me absolutely certain of my interpretation and I am sure that it could not have escaped any hunter who reads me. He says, in fact, that Paulus Amilius gave his son Scipio "liberty to hunt as much as he wanted." That is, exactly as today, the owner of the preserve could not take the luxury of granting carte blanche, but could only give limited licenses for a certain number of animals. The exception was so extraordinary that Polybius feels that he has to mention it.

To avoid complicating the text further, I take advantage of this footnote to point out that in both the quotation from the *Amadis* and the one from Polybius, when the subject of hunting comes up, the problem of "occupation" is automatically mentioned: "...*free* from other things that were more important to his position" (*Amadis*); "*preoccupied* with things of greater importance Perseus did not bother to hunt" (Polybius). The parallelism is perfect. And this is the heart of the matter. Therefore I have dedicated the first part of this text to it.

** For example, one item that sums up many others and has statistical precision: Pharaoh Amenophis III, who ruled about 1400 B.C.—therefore, a man who had one of the best opportunities to hunt beasts—had a memorial scarabaeus carved to boast of the feat of having hunted 102 lions in ten years of his reign. These hunts must have taken place in Asia Minor (*Reallexikon der Vorgeschichte*, vol. VI, p. 144). Another fact that can be used as a standard of measure is that given us by Alfonso de Palencia in his Cronica de Enrique IV (*op. cit.*). In the history of Spain Henry IV was the hunting king *par excellence*. His younger brother Antonio rebelled against him and proclaimed himself king. Yet, the only thing Henry could not forgive his brother was that one day Antonio killed forty deer in the

remains of some 10,000 wild horses* have been found in what is perhaps
the largest known field of prey(?)—the region around Solutré, which
gave its name to the Solutrean period, immediately before the
Magdalenian to which the paintings at Altamira belong. In the
Drachenhöle (Cavern of Dragons) in Styria, says Obermaier, document-
ing himself with the great Othenius Abel, 30,000 to 50,000 skeletons of
cave-dwelling bears were piled up, dead not at the hands of hunters but
due to natural causes. This is too many bears, is it not?

But at once we recall that the prehistorians use a chronology that
walks on very tall stilts. They speak of millennia as if they were nothing.
The durations of which they speak, like those of astronomers, are
expressed in such large figures that the whole beauty of numbers evaporates, becoming mere convention. In fact, to the aforementioned data
about the bears, Obermaier immediately adds, "Since more than five or
six families never lived together at the same time in the cave, it is to be
assumed that the Drachenhöle was the constant dwelling place of these
animals for more than 10,000 years."** The highly respected Obermaier
is now being reasonable. But if we take the smaller figure, as would be
sane, the 30,000 divide up into three bears a year. This is too few bears:
it is what I call the scarcity of game.

To gauge the quantity of game which presumably existed in the
Paleolithic Age, the documents which the hunters of that time left us in
their rock figurations are, for many problematic reasons, more important
than these facts. This is because those exciting images were put there,
paralyzed in stone, not for love of art, but rather for a magical purpose.
Primitive man is not yet practiced in abstracting and distinguishing;
everything *which has to do* with something he confuses with the thing

carefully guarded preserve in Segovia where he had about *three thousand deer* (see the
translation by Paz y Meliá, vol. II, p. 109). Philip IV (1605–1665), by the time he was
thirty-nine, had killed 400 wolves, 600 deer, and even more buck, 150 wild boar. For
sheer numbers it is a record. See Alfonso Martinez de Espinar, *Arte de Ballestería y
Montería* [Art of Archery and Hunting] (Madrid, 1644).

    * Lindner, *op. cit.*, p. 192.

    ** H. Obermaier and Antonio Garcia y Bellido, *El hombre prehistórico y los orígenes
de la humanidad* (Madrid: Revista de Occidente, 1941). 2nd ed., p. 22.

itself. Of course, this happens to contemporary man too—if not to the same degree, three-quarters of the way—and I have been toiling here for some time to keep us from confusing the hunt itself with that which merely *has to do* with it. Well, if there is anything that has to do with a thing it is its image and its name. Therefore, to the primitive, to possess the image and the name is, in a word, already to possess the thing itself. By covering the walls with drawings of animals, ritually consecrated, he believes he assures their presence in the environs. By drawing an arrow in the flank of an image, a successful hunt is already prefigured.

But this magic was not only meant to achieve success in wounding the prey, it was also "fertility magic." The figurative rite was performed so that the animal would be abundant and its females fertile.

This reminds me that many years ago in Madrid there was an exhibition of rock paintings, or rather of very neat copies of them. On that occasion, Francisco Alcantara, one of the most extraordinary men Spain has known and not appreciated in the last century, told me the following: He had entered the exhibition accompanied by a peasant, one of those pure-blooded Spaniards who used to come to see him from the farthest and most unlikely corners of the peninsula, people who smelled of rock-rose and lavender. The man came from the mountains near Avila, where he had lived his whole life among the wild cattle that produce the best veal in the world. Arriving in front of one of the prehistoric paintings of bison, suddenly, as if carried away, the old mountain cowhand exclaimed, "Damn, how real that cow looks giving birth!" One of the most incredible figures at Altamira is, in fact, in a position which I have never seen explained. Those devilish Cantabrian painters had such an extraordinary gift of observation and they lived so obsessed with animals that they could very well have wanted to represent there, practicing "fertility magic," a bison cow in the act of giving birth.

I do not really know whether this is actually what is happening, because, poor me, I have never seen a cow giving birth. But maybe it would not be a waste of time for Obermaier to consider the matter a moment, for which he would need to have witnessed previously the wonderful scene of a bovine birth.

The important thing—and what has motivated this reference to paleolithic magic—is that its existence constitutes the most unimpeachable and ample proof that game was not abundant in those millennia either. For it is clear that if it had been abundant, plentiful to the hunter, it neither would have occurred to him, nor would he have thought it necessary, to turn to a laborious rite to assure its presence and its future multiplication.

It would be appropriate to state precisely the three purposes of "hunting magic": (1) that there be a lot of game; (2) given that it exists, that the hunter find it; (3) once found, that the techniques used to capture it—the trap, driving it off a cliff, the dart, the arrow—function successfully. With the first purpose the primitive hunter makes a formal and explicit confession to us that he did not believe game to abound, so that for him the first act of hunting consists in procuring the existence of game, which apparently on its own was simply neither plentiful nor constant. For him—and the same goes for the "paleolithics" that still live today, in Australia, Ceylon, Sumatra, in Africa (the Bushmen), in the Andaman Islands—to perform the magic rite is already to begin to hunt; it is, in effect, "magic beating for game."

But the other two purposes implicitly declare just as much that this hunter, and without realizing it all past and future hunters, starts from the unquestionable assumption, unspoken because it is obvious, that the desired animal is uncommon. If it were plentiful there would be no question of not running into it, no problems and hardships of seeking it. If it is unnecessary to look for it because it is always at hand, in inexhaustible supply, one does not worry either about success in killing or capturing it. If the first blow fails, it is all the same; another animal is right at hand to receive a second aggression, and so on indefinitely.

But this last inference, which is of superlative simplicity and if well understood would seem to be an inane platitude, leads to a sudden realization. It dawns upon us that all this arduous proof, by means of concrete facts and adjunct reasoning, that the "scarcity of game" is a fact throughout human history, including prehistory, is completely unnecessary; we could have saved ourselves the trouble "without going out of the house," with a simple reflection on the very idea of the hunt.

For hunting is not simply casting blows right and left in order to kill animals or to catch them. The hunt is a series of technical operations, and for an activity to become technical it has to matter that it works in one particular way and not in another. Technique presupposes that success in reaching a certain goal is difficult and improbable; to compensate for its difficulty and improbability one must exert oneself to invent a special procedure of sufficient effectiveness. If we take one by one the different acts that comprise hunting, starting with the last—killing or capturing the prey and continuing backward toward the initial operation, we will see that they all presuppose the scarcity of game. The term used in big-game hunting, "*jugarse el lance,*"* is very indicative of what I am saying. It is the culminating moment in the hunting process: *finally* the prey appears at an adequate distance. But an instant later it will have gone, will have disappeared, and, *very likely, another will not appear*. Anybody who has hunted will recognize that each prey, when it "appears," seems as if it is going to be the only one. It is a flash of opportunity that one must take advantage of. For that reason it is called *lance. Perhaps* the occasion will not present itself again all day. Thus the excitement, always new, always fresh, even in the oldest hunter. But all this *presupposes* that achieving the presence of game is a triumph in itself, and very unusual good fortune. But how many efforts are necessary in order to have this fortunate opportunity, as instantaneous as a lightning flash, take place! The chain of venatic operations unfolds now before our retrospective analysis. And each technique is revealed as a difficult and ingenious effort to force the appearance of the animal, which apparently on his own will characteristically *not be there*. So, leaving aside the magic used by the primitives of the glacial period and their counterparts still living, the first act of all hunting is to find the prey and to "raise" it. Strictly speaking, this is not merely the first task, but rather the fundamental task of all hunting: bringing about the presence of the prey.

The "paleolithic" tribes of the present those that live, like those of 10,000 years ago, exclusively or almost exclusively by hunting represent the most primitive human species that exists. They do not have the slightest hint of government, of legislation, of authority; only one "law" is enforced among them: that which determines how they must divide the spoils of their hunting. In many of these tribes the largest and best portion of the spoils is given not to the one who kills, but rather to the

* *Jugarse*, to gamble or risk; *el lance*, the opportunity, the chance, the shot, the throw, the move.—Trans.

one who first saw the animal, discovered it and caused it to rise and show itself. It is almost certain that this was the "constitutional right" of hunting in the dawn of humanity. That is, when the history of hunting began, detecting the animal was already held to be the basic operation; therefore, the scarcity of game is of the essence of the whole undertaking. There is no more eminent proof that this initial labor is the most important part of hunting, and it is understandable that a very accomplished hunter should consider the supreme form of hunting that in which the hunter, alone in the mountains, is at the same time the person who discovers the prey, the one who pursues it, and the one who fells it. What happens is that the task turns out to be too hard, and usually it is better to divide the labor, to disassociate the one who finds the beast from the one who kills it. It is that difficult to find game! The same thing happens in hunting among animals, except that their techniques are gradually acquired by instinct and remain stereotyped in the species.

So we have come to a monumental but inevitable paradox: *the fact that man hunts presupposes that there is and always has been a scarcity of game*. If game were superabundant there would not exist that peculiar animal behavior which we distinguish from all others with the precise name "hunting." Since air is usually abundant, there is no technical ability involved in breathing, and breathing is not hunting air.

I hope nobody presents the objection that in such and such a place and on such and such a date a gigantic accumulation of animals was seen. Those who traveled through certain regions of Africa a century ago speak of herds of antelopes in close formation that took several days to pass in front of the hunter. Apart from the exaggeration in this story, it is clear that such facts only serve to confirm our thesis. In fact, we are talking about enormous concentrations of animals, which are due to those animals' having evacuated immense areas. There are many together in one spot precisely because there are none scattered about elsewhere. Abnormal causes—terrible droughts, plagues that impoverish the pastures, vast fires—impose on the beasts those migratory movements of a pathological character. The concentration prevents them from finding sufficient food, and the fabulous interminable processions end in the death of almost all the individuals.

It is contrary to my purpose to enter now into a study of specious arguments because a superficial reflection quickly reduces them to a general rule. For example, there are animals which are produced and live *only* in agglomeration, such as sardines, which form "schools." An animal—whether the fisherman or the voracious dogfish—that encounters the school has only to throw a net or to open his mouth to draw in fish to satiety. But, and this is the problem, how do you find the school of sardines? Their fabulous accumulation in one spot is due to their absence from all others, so that hunting or fishing these multitudinous animals consists more than anything else in the problem of finding their whereabouts.*

The words "scarcity" and "abundance" in the usual hunting vocabulary have a merely relative meaning which tacitly assumes the prey's never greatly abounding; thus in the absolute sense of the term, the game is always scarce. Now it is clear why I said before that the idea of privilege is related to the idea of hunting. To avoid exaggerating in front of the poorly prepared reader I said then, as an extreme, that in the Neolithic period the hunt must already have adopted certain privileged forms. But the truth is even more radical. Obermaier says that in the most primitive period, in the period even earlier than Altamira, each human tribe had marked out its own region.** So at least the territorial privilege existed, or the so-called privilege "of utilization" in a territory. It could not have been otherwise, given the scarcity of animals that always existed.

---

* The case of the sardine, the fishing of which is today purely utilitarian, offers the best example, because no way yet has been found to discover the law that governs the movement of their "schools." For some years they are found in certain waters. Costly factories for preserving and salting are created in nearby ports. But one fine day the school disappears, without anyone's knowing where it has gone. After some time it reappears 600 or 1000 miles farther down the coast. In 1900, the great school of Atlantic sardines was off the coast of Galicia; today [1942] it is off southern Portugal. But as I revise this text the newspapers are publishing news of the school's reappearance off the Galician coast.

** Obermaier (*op. cit.*) gives a very penetrating and precise reason for this belief: only this limitation of the hunt to a particular region, which obliged the tribe, on the other hand, to isolate itself in it, can explain the stylistic differences between the utensils within zones which are not large at all. This is amusing: when man excluded others from his hunting ground, when he marked out a territory, he marked out himself and his culture. See Lindner, *op. cit.*, p. 380, for more on this subject.

However, do not confuse the fact that "game has always been scarce" with the evident diminishing that has been observed in the last hundred years and which was our point of departure for the preceding analysis. Now it is a question of extreme and rapidly advancing scarcity. Now it is a matter of fewer animals each day. Now it is a matter of a dramatic reality: that the game is disappearing, that hunting is dying, that soon man will have to stop being a hunter, and that this outstanding form of his happiness is on the verge of vanishing. More and greater efforts keep being made to counteract that decline: better hunting laws and greater rigor in their enforcement, creation of parks and sanctuaries for animals; but all this does not succeed in checking the rest of human progress, which, as it continues "humanizing" the planet, takes away from it, like it or not, the spontaneity of Nature. These efforts succeed the hard way in maintaining the survival of some animals, but at the cost of so many precautions and so much wit that the occupation of hunting has been made much too artificial and has lost its most exquisite flavor: the rough wildness of hunting country and the illusion of going through struggles in regions where "civilization"—that is to say, other men, the *civitas*, the law, the state—does not reach. Hunting is thus limited to its two least appealing ingredients: climbing mountains and shooting at a target. Pushed by reason, man is condemned to make progress, and this means that he is condemned to go farther and farther away from Nature, to construct in its place an artificial Nature. Now it is clear why I said earlier that, far from hunting's being a "reasoned pursuit" of the animal, the greatest enemy of hunting is reason.*

The error of believing that it is feasible to save game stems from the same root that sustains the belief that "before, it was plentiful," and this root is the false idea that we have of those animal species associated with our human species in a hunting relationship. We imagine them endowed with an imposing biological resistance. The urbanized and cultivated man has almost always felt a funny snobbery toward anything wild, man

---

* It would take us too far off the track to enumerate here all the ways and methods in which, without meaning to, human reason is gradually destroying the possibility of there being game and hunting.

or animal. In some periods this snobbery erupts violently, as in the wild romanticism which suddenly carried away Rousseau and the marquises of Versailles, and after them, all of Europe. Even today, in the cities it is believed that the country man is more vigorous than the man from the deleterious boroughs. But this is not true. From the noble wild animal living in the desert steppes to the long-billed woodcock of the calm waters, all species that matter to the hunter—with the only exception, perhaps, the rabbit, which is a semidomestic animal—are of extreme biological instability. Any circumstance can upset their vitality and exterminate them. For this reason their location has always been very much circumscribed by precise conditions of climate, land, and altitude. They lack the fabulous flexibility of man that allows him to adapt himself to all circumstances, so that the very wise father Teilhard* has been able to give man's near-planetary ubiquity as one of the merely zoological attributes that distinguish him from the other animals. There are men in the tropics and the polar circles, at an altitude of 4000 meters (Bolivia) and below sea level (Holland). We call ourselves neurasthenic, but the truth is that the real neurasthenics are found among the wild animals. "Melancholy flowed through his heart," Cervantes says of Don Quixote with clinical precision when, conquered by the Knight of the White Moon, he finds the world faded and, spirits flagging, he leans toward death. But that melancholy is not so bad in comparison with the melancholy of the orangutan, which dies of sadness as soon as his surroundings are changed. For this reason it is almost impossible to keep this animal in captivity.

There is no reason to blame our deadly weapons exclusively or principally for the disappearance of game, as is usually done when one is speaking, for example, of the North American bison or buffalo. This great magnificent animal, with its appearance of vital prepotency, existed in enormous herds and in one century has disappeared. Doubtless bullets contributed exceedingly to this deplorable destiny. But it was not only the bullets....I referred just now to the sensibility of the Marquise de Pompadour—well, the most decisive and fatal fact in the history of the

* Pierre Teilhard de Chardin (1881–1955).—Trans.

American buffalo was its move from the prairies on the eastern shore of the Mississippi River to the opposite shore. To what was this due? To the terrible hunters? No. The circumstances were these. The first pioneers who arrived on the prairies brought cows that gently grazed the high grass of the plains daily; as is customary, to avoid losing the cows, the pioneers hung bells from their docile necks. In the late afternoon, in the slanting rays of the dying sun, they grazed slowly, and as they walked the tender music of the cowbells sounded, like soft teardrops of sound falling on the countryside. But this lyrical noise completely upset the buffalo's idea of the world and produced in these magnificent beasts such anxiety and nervousness, and in the end such great fear, that, crazed, tens of thousands threw themselves into the river and swam to the other side.* Now who laughs at Madame de Pompadour!

---

* Washington Irving tells about this in his *Tour of the Prairies*, published about 1834. [Ortega is wrong here on two counts: the geographical distribution of the buffalo and the cause of its virtual extinction. For a more correct picture, see Martin S. Garretson, *The American Bison* (New York: New York Zoological Society, 1938).— Trans.]

Suddenly We Hear the Sound of Barking

The need to underline the essential scarcity of game, a presupposition in all hunting, has obliged us to go through so many circumlocutions that the principal idea has disappeared from sight; we have lost track of what motivated our discussion in the first place. It seems that, as in the old ballad,

We lost Don Beltran
In the great cloud of dust.

Let us renew the guidelines of our trajectory. Hunting is, then, clearly a relationship between two animals of different zoological level, a relationship in which two systems of instincts confront each other: the aggressive instincts of the hunter and the defensive instincts of the game. All means of pursuit and capture which the hunter employs correspond to countermeasures of evasion that the prey employs. But usually we are only aware of the least effective of these defensive countermeasures, since they are the most obvious: swiftness and agility which facilitate flight; a highly developed sense of smell, which alerts the animal; perceptive sight, which scrutinizes the horizon. All this would be of little value to the beast without another general countermeasure which penetrates and gives form to his entire life: his ability to keep himself hidden, which, among other things, has taught the beast nocturnal habits. But, in turn and in the end, hiding would be inefficient and illusory if it were not automatically helped a great deal by the very scarcity of the animal. Everything begins with this fact; it is necessary to begin with it if one wants truly to understand the peculiar task called hunting.

Reinforced, then, by the relative rarity of the animal, his instincts for hiding make his being absent the greatest problem that the venatic art has to solve. Every hunter knows that, with regard to the animal, what he has to fight most is the beast's absence. Thus the principal theme of hunting turns out to be the initial theme: the detection of the game. And this is so difficult that it has always claimed the greatest efforts on the part of the hunter. But the supreme effort made by man to resolve this problem, which I repeat is at once the principal and the initial problem in hunting, was not a physical effort but a mental one. This effort has caused him to promote the only substantial progress there has been, and could have been, in the history of hunting.

In fact, in order to check the supreme instinct of the animal, which is to make himself invisible, man does not have another counterinstinct. If he had such an instinct in his prehuman stage, he has lost it together with all the rest, or at best he conserves only rudiments of it. For its part, reason, which came to fill the gap left by the evanescent instincts, fails in the task of raising the suspicious game. For millennia man gave this difficulty a magical solution, and therefore no solution at all. But one day he had an ingenious inspiration, and in order to discover the extremely cautious animal he resorted to the detective instinct of another animal; he asked for its help. This is the point at which the dog was introduced into hunting, the only effective progress imaginable in the chase, consisting, not in the direct exercise of reason, but rather in man's accepting reason's insufficiency and placing another animal between his reason and the game.

This would have been impossible if the dog had not already hunted on his own account. Man has done no more than correct the dog's instinctive style of hunting, molding it to the convenience of a collaboration. The knowledge of this fact, so central to man's hunting activities, should have been enough to prevent anyone's ever isolating man completely from animal hunting in general by attributing an excessive role to reason, making something totally new of this human occupation. Here is the dog, which has always been an enthusiastic hunter on his own initiative. Thanks to that, man integrates the dog's hunting into his own and so raises hunting to its most complex and perfect form. This achievement was to hunting what the discovery of polyphony was to music. In fact, with the addition of dogs to beaters and shooters, hunting acquires a certain kind of symphonic majesty.

Up to that point nothing happens in the countryside. The chains of sleep still weigh upon hunters. The beaters cross lazily, still mute and joyless. One would say that no one had the desire to hunt. Everything is still static. The scenery is still purely vegetal and therefore paralytic. At most, the furze, heather, and thyme tremble slightly in the comb of the morning wind. There are some other movements of a cinematic nature, lacking the dynamism that would reveal governing forces. Wandering birds fly slowly toward some easy task. Faster, musical insects glide near the hunter's ear humming their aria of microscopic violins. The hunter withdraws into himself. Things are said at that time, of course, stupid things which lead him to close himself off more. He does nothing. He does not want to do anything. The sudden immersion in the countryside has numbed and annulled him. He feels himself a plant, a botanical entity, and he surrenders himself to that which in the animal is almost vegetal: breathing. But here they come, here comes the pack, and instantly the whole horizon is charged with a strange electricity; it begins to move, to stretch elastically. Suddenly the orgiastic element shoots forth, the dionysiac, which flows and boils in the depths of all hunting. Dionysios is the hunting god: "skilled cynegetic," Euripides calls him in *The Bacchantes*. "Yes, yes," answers the chorus, "the god is a hunter!" There is a universal vibration. Things that before were inert and flaccid have suddenly grown nerves, and they gesticulate, announce, foretell. There it is, there's the pack! Thick saliva, panting, chorus of jaws, and the arcs of tails excitedly whipping the countryside! The dogs are hard to restrain; their desire to hunt consumes them, pouring from eyes, muzzle, and hide. Visions of swift beasts pass before their excited eyes, while, within, they are already in hot pursuit.

There is another long pause of silence and immobility. But now the quiet is filled by restrained motion, as the scabbard is filled by the sword. In the distance the first cries of the beaters sound. In the hunter's eyes nothing has changed, and yet he seems to be feeling, though not actually seeing, a latent restlessness in the plains: quick movements from thicket to thicket, indecisive flights, and all the small mountain fauna stiffen, prick up their ears, and watch. Without his meaning it to, the hunter's soul leaps out, spreads out over the hunting ground like a net, anchored here and there with the fingernails of his attention. Now everything is imminent and at any instant any figure of the countryside can become— as if by magic—the hunter's prey.

Suddenly a dog's bark shatters the prevailing silence. This bark is not merely a point of noise that appears at a spot on the mountain and remains there—rather it seems to extend rapidly in a line. We hear, and almost see, the barking run loose, weaving swiftly through space like some erratic star. In an instant the barking runs over the plains like a lightning bolt. Many different voices follow it, advancing in the same way. The game is seen, raised in dizzying flight like wind on the wind. The entire countryside is polarized, seemingly magnetized. The fear of the pursued animal is like a vacuum into which everything in the environs is thrown. Beaters, dogs, small game, everything heads that way, and even the birds, frightened, fly rapidly in that direction. The fear which causes the beast to flee absorbs the entire countryside, suctions it, carries it racing along behind, and even the hunter, outwardly quiet, is inwardly moved, his heart racing wildly. The beast's fear...but is it so certain that the beast is afraid? At least his fear is not at all like fear in man. In the animal fear is permanent; it is his way of life, his occupation. We are talking, then, about a professional fear, and when something becomes professionalized it is quite different. Therefore, while fear makes man slow of mind and movement, it carries the faculties of the beast to their greatest performance. Animal life culminates in fear. Skillfully the stag eludes the obstacle; with millimetric precision he threads swiftly through the gap between two tree trunks. Nose to the wind, neck arched, he lets swing free the regal antlery which balances his acrobatics, as the pole does for the tightrope walker. He gains distance with the speed of a meteor. His hoofs hardly touch the ground; rather, as Nietzsche says of the dancer, he limits himself to acknowledging it with the point of his foot; acknowledging it in order to eliminate it, in order to leave it behind. Suddenly, on the spine of a low ridge the stag appears to the hunter; he sees him cut across the sky with the elegant grace of a constellation, launched there by the springs of his slender extremities. The leap of roe deer or stag—and even more of certain antelopes—is perhaps the most beautiful event that occurs in Nature. He lands again at a distance and accelerates his flight, because the snorting dogs are close on his heels—the dogs, abettors of all this vertigo, that have transmitted their delightful frenzy to the mountain and now, in pursuit of the game, tongues hanging out, bodies stretched to their full length, gallop obsessed—hound, mastiff, beagle, greyhound.

The dog enters domesticity toward the end of the Paleolithic Age, in the later Capsian culture, contemporaneous with the Solutrean-Magdalenian. Its first documented appearance is found in Spain, in the Cave of the Old Woman of Alpera. It seems that it was not yet used in hunting. This happens a little later, at the beginning of the Neolithic Age, in the period called Maglemosian. The dog was, then, the first domestic animal. It is not even certain that man domesticated it; certain evidence suggests that the dog spontaneously approached man. Doubtless the leavings of food attracted him. Perhaps, even more than food, the dog found something else attractive in being close to man: warmth. It is enough to see the happiness of today's dog when he is beside a fire. The coals intoxicate him, and do not forget that man is, first and foremost, the animal with fire in his fist.* The manipulation of fire, the success of having it at his disposal, was man's first physical discovery and the root of all the others. Before anything else he dominated flame; he arises in Nature as the flammiferous beast.

It is a shame that the enigmas of domestication have not yet been cleared up a little. In the Paleolithic Age and the beginnings of the Neolithic, during a relatively brief period, man domesticated a series of animal species. Since then he has not been able to add even one to those that he domesticated in that time. On the contrary, some species that were tamed turned wild again later. Domesticated hyenas and leopards appear in the oldest Egyptian drawings.** The genius of domestication is, then, circumscribed within a specific stage of human evolution. It is a talent which man had and later lost. So much for man. On the animal's side there is the following, the principal aspect of which I have never seen pointed out.

---

* The other animal that was to look for a way of life near man, and perhaps for the same incandescent reason, is the bee.
** In some corners of Asia, nevertheless, men still hunt with leopards.

From the zoological point of view, the domesticated animal is a degenerate one, as is man himself. In the artificial existence which man offers, the beast loses not a few of his instincts, even though he refines others which man needs and tries to select in breeding. The space left in the animal's life by the loss of these instincts is filled by teaching and training. But generally this is something that is only trivially and superficially understood. Through training man introduces certain forms of human conduct in the animal. That is, domestication partially de-animalizes and partially humanizes the beast. This is to say that *the domestic animal is an intermediate reality between the pure animal and man*, which, in turn, is to say that *something like* reason operates in the domestic animal. That is what has never been pointed out, although it is completely obvious.*

An eminent example of this is the bark. Almost no hunter is aware that barking is not natural in dogs. Neither the wild dog nor the species from which it proceeds—wolf, jackal—barks, rather they simply howl. Finally to confirm this fact we possess the evidence of the intermediate stage: the oldest domestic dogs, certain American and Australian breeds, are mute. Remember the surprise with which Columbus, in the report of his first voyage, noted that the dogs of the Antilles did not bark. These dogs had stopped howling and had not yet learned to bark.**

The difference between the howl and the bark is a radical one. The howl is comparable to man's cry of pain, an expressive "gesture." Through it, as through the other spontaneous gestures, the subject's emotional state is manifested. The word, on the other hand, in so far as it is

---

* This is not the place to discuss the question fully, but it concerns an old idea of mine that seems important and fertile to me, and I do not want to fail to mention it here, briefly at least, in case I do not have the time or the opportunity to develop it later. It would lead to experiments in which the behavior of domestic animals was compared to that of their savage varieties or proximate species. This would reveal with sufficient precision an advanced state in the domestic animal in the process from Nature to man. This would have a double advantage: it would permit us to understand the pure animal (predomestic) better, and, on the other hand, it would contribute a little to the clarification of how the "humanoid" humanized himself, how reason emerged in him. It must be noted that on the anatomical side the parallelism is unquestionable. In the domestic dog the anterior cerebrum has developed extraordinarily, while in the wild dog the development has occurred in the posterior cerebrum. Exactly the same relationship is found in comparing the cranium of *Homo primigenius* (Neanderthal) and present-day European man.

** Modern scientific observations do not bear out Ortega's theory. Wolves and jackals do bark, and the muteness he refers to may be the result of training.—Trans.

strictly a word, expresses nothing; rather it has meaning, it signifies something.* Comparably, it happens that the howl and the scream are involuntary, and when not involuntary, they are feigned, imitated. One cannot *want* to give an authentic "scream of fright"; one can only wish to repress it. Words, on the other hand, are not emitted except voluntarily. That is why howling and screaming are not speech. Well then, barking is an elementary form of speech. When a stranger passes by a farmhouse, the dog barks, not because anything hurts him, but because "he wishes to tell" his master that a stranger is near. And the master, if he is acquainted with his dog's "dictionary" can learn more details: the passerby's disposition; whether he is passing nearby or far away; if he is alone or in a group, and something I find frightful, whether the traveler is rich or poor. Through domestication, therefore, the dog has acquired in his bark a quasi-language, and this implies that a quasi-reason has begun to germinate in him.

Notice how admirably well informed is the old saying that the Spanish mountain people use to describe the barking of the pack. They call it "talking." The veteran hunter finally learns perfectly the rich vocabulary and the subtle grammar of this canine quasi-language.

Man and dog have articulated in each other their own styles of hunting, and this represents the height of hunting. Cynegetics—hunting with dogs—has become the perfect example of the art, so much so that the proper meaning of the term cynegetics has finally been applied to the entire art of the hunt, whatever its forms may be.** The qualification of the dog for hunting, once achieved, was an invitation to generalize the procedure, and, in fact, man tried to involve other animals in his hunting. Nevertheless, he only achieved it in a very reduced and rather sad form

---

* A certain contraction of the facial muscles *expresses* our sadness. The word "sadness," on the other hand, signifies that sentimental reality that takes hold of us at times. But "sadness," as a word, does not express our sadness or anyone else's: it is not "sad" as is that gesture of the features. When *said* by someone, happy or sad, the word "sadness" always has the same meaning. The sad person would include in his pronunciation of it something of a moan, and the happy person something of laugh, and this—the way in which the same word is pronounced—is all the expression it has.

** It would be better, nevertheless, to discourage this usage, because it turns out to be too ridiculous to call cynegetic an activity in which the dog often does not take part. An opposite error is committed by many hunters when they believe that the venatic art is so called because in exercising it venison stags are often caught. The truth is the contrary. *Venado—venatu*—signifies simply "the game." But since a certain species of stag is the ideal game for the hunter, its meaning contracted. *Venado*, then, means the hunted—that

with the ferret, and in a broader and more glorious form with the bird of prey.* Cynegetics has its counterpart in falconry or hunting with hawks. The bird of prey is also a great hunter on his own. Of course, his style is very different from that of the dog. These heraldic birds are austere, ill-tempered gentlemen who maintain themselves at a distance like marquises of old, so that it is not possible to become intimate with them. Their domestication was always precarious. They continued to be beasts. The bird, in general, is not intelligent enough and does not have enough plasticity. To know this one has only to notice the rigidity of its corporeal form, which makes the bird an inexpressive, geometric, hieratic animal. This does not take away from the fact that, up close, birds of prey are perhaps the most imposing figures in all zoology. The flat and well-combed head of the eagle, just a lever for the inexorable beak, has always been the emblem of empire. The eye of the falcon, all pupil, is the hunting eye *par excellence*, the alert eye. The bird of prey—goshawk, falcon gentle, gerfalcon—is, as authentic aristocrats usually are, somber, hard, and a hunter.

But before man hunted with the real bird of flesh and blood, he had already invented the mechanical bird. It would fit well into the intellectual scheme of early man, if, as is not unlikely, the arrow represented a materialized metaphor. When the hunter saw the animal gallop off out of his reach he thought that a bird with its light wings might be able to catch up to it. Since he was not a bird and did not have one handy—it is sur-

is, the game *par excellence*. If some hunter is an *aficionado* of linguistics and is amused at splitting hairs, it would be most interesting to investigate the strange fact that the Latin verb "to hunt"—*venor*—is a deponent verb, at least in its principal usage. Since hunting is not just an action, but one of the most transitive actions that one can imagine, how is it that Latin employs a passive form, or more exactly, a "middle voice"? The middle voice is that which announces an activity which affects the very subject that performs it; therefore a reflexive action. "To fall asleep," "to move oneself," would be then "middle voice." But, *venari*, could it have meant "to hunt oneself"? That way, the game would be its own hunter in the hunt...Or perhaps *venor* means "I hunt partridges for myself"? This does not make sense and this is the riddle, which has a lot of meat to it, so much so that it is worth our while to avoid it now so that we will not get indigestion. Our curiosity grows when we find that in Greek *thereuo*, "to hunt," is a normal verb, but that Plato and Aristotle use it in middle voice.

* In individual cases it has been possible to instruct many other animals in the task of hunting with and for man, but it has not been possible to consolidate this practice in the species.

prising how little attention primitive man paid to birds—he put a beak on one end of a stick and feathers on the other; that is, he created the artificial bird, the arrow, which flies swiftly through the air toward the flanks of the fleeing great stag.*

* In the Lower Paleolithic Age—that is, the earliest—the arrow had not yet appeared. The preponderant fauna in that period were the great pachyderms, much larger than the present-day elephant and rhinoceros, even larger than the mammoth. Even if the arrow had existed it would have been of little use. But in the Upper Paleolithic Age, and especially in its last stage, the fauna were bovine, cervine, and equine: the bison, the aurochs or great savage bull, the wild horse, the wild ass, the red deer. Then the arrow appeared. In Jyderup [Denmark] an aurochs's skeleton was found with three quartz-headed arrows stuck in it. I believe—but the reader should not trust this too much—that the Stone Age art of the Spanish Levant is where the arrow appears for the first time. From Spain it went north to the rest of Europe.

The Ethics
of
Hunting

At this point we arrive at the terminus, the goal of hunting itself. And although this goal or final scene is sometimes the capture of the animal, its most frequent and natural form is the death of the beast. Death, especially "caused" death, murder, is or should be a terrifying thing. The hunter does not just come and go, working hard in valleys and on cliffs, urging on his dogs; rather, in the last analysis, he kills. The hunter is a death dealer.

The mission of thought is to construct archetypes; I mean, to point out from among the infinite figures that reality presents those in which, because of their greater purity, that reality becomes clearer. Once understood in its exemplary form, the reality is also elucidated in its obscure, confused, and deficient forms, and these are the more frequent forms. A person who has never seen a good bullfight cannot understand what the mediocre and awful ones are. This is because bad bullfights, which are almost all of them, exist only at the expense of the good ones, which are very unusual. In the human order at least, the depraved, the stupid, and the trivial are tenacious parasites of perfection. Don't fret about it; the harmful doctor lives thanks to the eminent one, and if there are so many bad writers it is because there have been some good ones.

The exemplary moral spirit of the sporting hunter, that manner of feeling, of taking up and practicing hunting, is a very precise line, below which fall innumerable forms of hunting that are deficient modes of this occupation; deficient in the aspects of dexterity, boldness, and effort, or simply in the moral aspect. Without doubt, above that line there is room for, and there do occur, greater refinements; but if we examine them carefully we will discover that they are mannerisms and excrescences. Hunting, like every human activity, has an ethic which distinguishes virtues from vices. There is such a thing as a rogue hunter, but there is also an affected piety of hunting.

All this leads up to that final scene of the hunt in which the fine skin of the animal appears stained with blood, and that body, once pure agility, lies transformed into the absolute paralysis that is death. Was it all only for this, we ask ourselves. More than once, the sportsman, within shooting range of a splendid animal, hesitates in pulling the trigger. The idea that such a slender life is going to be annulled surprises him for an instant. *Every good hunter is uneasy in the depths of his conscience when faced with the death he is about to inflict on the enchanting animal.* He does not have the final and firm conviction that his conduct is correct. But neither, it should be understood, is he certain of the opposite. Finding himself in an ambivalent situation which he has often wanted to clear up, he thinks about this issue without ever obtaining the sought-after evidence. I believe that this has always happened to man, with varying degrees of intensity according to the nature of the prey—ferocious or harmless—and with one or another variation in the aspect of uneasiness. This says nothing against hunting, but only that the generally problematic, equivocal nature of man's relationship with animals shines through that uneasiness. Nor can it be otherwise, because man has never really known exactly what an animal is. Before and beyond all science, humanity sees itself as something emerging from animality, but it cannot be sure of having transcended that state completely. The animal remains too close for us to not feel mysterious communication with it. The only people to have felt that they had a clear idea about the animal were the Cartesians. The truth is that they believed they had a clear idea about everything. But to achieve that rigorous distinction between man and beast, Descartes had first to convince himself that the animal was a mineral—that is, a mere machine. Fontenelle recounts that in his youth, while he was visiting Malebranche, a pregnant dog came into the room. So that it would not disturb anyone who was present, Malebranche—a very sweet and somewhat sickly priest, whose spine was twisted like a corkscrew—had the dog expelled with blows from a stick. The poor animal ran away howling piteously, while Malebranche, a Cartesian, listened impassively. "It doesn't matter," he said. "It's a machine, it's a machine!"

In a truly exhaustive study of hunting I would feel obliged to delve profoundly into that dimension of its ethics which inflicting death on the animal makes inevitable. But I restrain myself because the theme is enormously difficult. There is, first of all, the unbelievable backwardness and coarseness that characterizes studies of morality. Next to the atrocity of the demagogues, the stupidity of the moralists, or their total absence, is the chief cause of the division that today afflicts the human community. There is greater confusion than ever with regard to the norms which ought to govern the relations between men, to say nothing of those which could orient and regulate our treatment of the other realities present in our environment: the mineral, the vegetable, and the animal. There are people who believe in good faith that we have no obligations toward the rocks and therefore have tolerated advertisers' smearing with pitch or white lead the venerable rocks of the mountain ranges, on which over the millennia the rains have woven prodigious covering of lichens and fungi.

A second difficulty lies in the fact that the ethics of death is the most difficult of all, because death is the least intelligible fact that man stumbles upon. In the morality of hunting, the enigma of death is multiplied by the enigma of the animal.

Finally, a third possibility is contained in the question. Death is enigmatic enough when it comes of itself, through sickness, old age, and debilitation. But it is much more so when it does not come spontaneously but instead is produced by another being. Assassination is the most disconcerting event that exists in the universe, and the assassin is the man that we never understand. Hence his bloody action has always demanded dreadful expiations and he himself has been expelled from the community. There still sound in our ears, perpetuated in the first pages of Genesis, atrocious screams that frighten us, horrible growls of a corralled beast. What we hear is the voice of Cain, the first murderer, the patron of all assassins. He has been condemned, and the God of Adam demands the fulfillment of the tribal law which expels the parricide: "What hast thou done? The voice of thy brother's blood cries unto me from the ground" (Genesis 4:10). Cain foresees the harshness of his future, wandering and without group protection, and he screams to God, crying out: "I shall be a fugitive and a vagabond in the earth, and it shall come to pass that everything that findeth me shall slay me" (Genesis 4:14).

Has anyone noticed the very strange fact that, before and apart from any moral or even simply compassionate reaction, it seems to us that nothing stains as blood does? When two men who have had a fistfight in the street finally separate and we see their bloodstained faces we are always disconcerted. Rather than producing in us the sympathetic response which another's pain generally causes, the sight creates a disgust which is extremely intense and of a very special nature. Not only do those faces seem repugnantly stained, but the filth goes beyond physical limits and becomes, at the same time, moral. The blood has not only stained the faces but it has soiled them—that is to say, it has debased and in a way degraded them. Hunters who read this will remember this primary sensation, so often felt, when at the end of the hunt the dead game lies in a heap on the ground, with dried blood here and there staining plumage and pelt. The reaction I repeat, is prior to and still deeper than any ethical question, since one notices the degradation that blood produces wherever it falls, on inanimate things as well. The earth that is stained with blood is as damned. A white rag stained with blood is not only repugnant, it seems violated, its humble textile material dishonored.* It is the frightening mystery of blood! What can it be? Life is the mysterious reality *par excellence*, not only in the sense that we do not know its secret but also because life is the only reality that has a true "inside"—an *intus* or intimacy. Blood, the liquid that carries and symbolizes life, is meant to flow occultly, secretly, through the interior of the body. When it is spilled and the essential "within" comes outside, a reaction of disgust and terror is produced in all Nature, as if the most radical absurdity had been committed: that which is purely internal made external.**

---

* Once more the etymology corroborates our intuition. The Spanish word *mancillar*, which means "to dishonor," comes from *macellare*, which means "to kill," and especially the activity of the butcher and the slaughterer. *Macellum* is the butchershop and slaughterhouse. Our moral *mancilla* [stain] carries within it nothing other than bloodiness. And the fact is that the Latin word represents an enormous cultural area, because it comes from a Greek word which in turn reproduces a Semitic word.

** Nevertheless, it is necessary to register with complete honesty the sinuosities and apparent caprices of reality. There is one case in which blood does not produce that disgust: when it spurts from the nape of a bull that has been lanced well (*picado*) and spills

But this is precisely what death is. The cadaver is flesh which has lost its intimacy, flesh whose "interior" has escaped like a bird from a cage, a piece of pure matter in which there is no longer anyone hidden.

Yet after this first bitter impression, if the blood insists on presenting itself, if it flows abundantly, it ends by producing the opposite effect: it intoxicates, excites, maddens both man and beast. The Romans went to the circus as they did to the tavern, and the bullfight public does the same: the blood of the gladiators, the beasts, the bull operates like a stupefying drug. Similarly, war is always an orgy at the time. Blood has an unequaled orgiastic power.

Is the reader beginning to see why it is impossible to go deeply into the ethics of hunting in this essay? When we reach the problem of death we become entangled in more complicated questions and would have to prolong indefinitely an essay of which the exuberance is already too tropical. I have said that the fact of spontaneous death, natural death, is already rather unintelligible in itself. There is, besides, the fact of killing, which multiplies the unintelligibility. But this pyramid of difficulties has yet a third level—namely, *having* to kill. At times killing the enemy, the madman, the criminal is obligatory and unavoidable. And many animal species, man among them, have no other recourse than to kill in order to eat. The result is that we not only have to suffer the presence of death around us, and through imaginative anticipation our own inevitable death, but we also have to produce it and manipulate it. The situation, then, is that when death is said to be horrible, very little has been said about it, because that adjective, like adjectives in general, resolves nothing. Nothing has been said about the fact that the greatest and most moral homage we can pay to certain animals on certain occasions is to kill them with certain means and rituals.

So hunting is counterposed to all that morphology of death as something without equal, since it is the only normal case in which the killing of one creature constitutes the delight of another. This raises to the last paroxysm the difficulties of its ethics.

---

down both sides of the animal. In the sun, the crimson of the brilliant liquid takes on a refulgence that turns it into a jewel. This exception, the only one that I know of, is as strange as the rule that it breaks.

The English have initiated a form of hunting in which all these conflicts of conscience are cleverly eluded: it is a matter of having the hunt end, not with the capture or death of the animal, but rather with taking the game's picture. What a refinement! Don't you think so? What tenderness of soul these Anglo-Saxons have! One feels ashamed that one day, at siesta time thirty years ago, one killed that overly impertinent fly! Of course the British Empire was not forged with silks and bonbons, but by employing the greatest harshness Western man has ever seen in the face of the suffering of other men.

This reminds me that in the darkest moment of the Spanish civil war an Englishwoman, or a woman raised in England, offered money for ambulances to gather the wounded and to care for them. The offer was accepted, but when it came to carrying out the plan, it turned out that the wounded for whom the woman had intended the ambulances were not men wounded in the war but injured or sick dogs. And the good woman said, "Men who make them are to blame for terrible wars, but dogs are not to blame for the injuries they receive." But how and for what reason was she so sure that men are ultimately to blame for wars? Why does this woman, who manipulates the apothegm like one of Plutarch's philosophers, have enough perceptiveness to discover the blamelessness of the dog and yet be completely blind to the ultimately doggish in man, lost in an existence that he does not dominate and cudgeled from the one side and another by the most impenetrable Destiny? Instead of worrying so much about dogs, she should have tried a little harder to be less sure about things which perhaps one can never be sure about. Under its appearance of ultrasensitive tenderness, that brutal sureness with regard to what is, absolutely or for the present, indiscernible represents a peculiar form of barbarism, nourished at the breasts of stupidity and petulance. I hope the reader will pardon this spontaneous outburst, but nothing in the universe irritates me as much as seeing people feel too sure of things where such sureness is impossible, and when this woman crossed my mind the pure mastiff that I may be ran out to bark at her. Just a few days ago I read in *The Times* news of the skirmish that another woman started in South Africa by suing an insurance company because they refused to guarantee the safety, in wartime, of the goldfish in her pools.

To the real brutality in the treatment of animals which was habitual in some Latin countries some years ago, the Englishman responds with another exaggeration.* Photographic hunting is a mannerism and not a refinement; it is an ethical mandarinism no less deplorable than the intellectual pose of the other mandarins. England, like all nations that have enjoyed good fortune for too long, had fallen into intensive mandarinism. The copious admiration that I feel for the strong English people makes me prefer their classic firmness to these recent mannered tendernesses. And such a preference is not purely my whim. In the preoccupation with doing things as they should be done—which is morality—there is a line past which we begin to think that what is purely our whim or mania is necessary. We fall, therefore, into a new immorality, into the worst of all, which is a matter of not knowing those very conditions without which things cannot be. This is man's supreme and devastating pride, which tends not to accept limits on his desires and supposes that reality lacks any structure of its own which may be opposed to his will. This sin is the worst of all, so much so that the question of whether the content of that will is good or bad completely loses importance in the face of it. If you believe that you can do whatever you like—even, for example, the supreme good, then you are, irretrievably, a villain. The preoccupation with what should be is estimable only when the respect for what is has been exhausted.

A good example of this, because of the very insignificance of its substance, is this ridiculousness of photographic hunting. One can refuse to hunt, but if one hunts one has to accept certain ultimate requirements** without which the reality "hunting" evaporates. The overpowering of the game, the tactile drama of its actual capture, and usually even more the tragedy of its death nurture the hunter's interest through anticipation and give liveliness and authenticity to all the previous work: the harsh confrontation with the animal's fierceness, the struggle with its energetic

---

* It is inconceivable that no study from the ethical point of view has ever been made of the Society for the Prevention of Cruelty to Animals, analyzing its standards and actions. I bet one would find that English zoophilia has one of its roots in a certain secret English antipathy toward everything human that is not either English or Ancient Greek!

** *Requirement* is the name that the philosopher Leibniz gave to the indispensable elements essential to every being.

defense, the point of orgiastic intoxication aroused by the sight of blood, and even the hint of criminal suspicion which claws the hunter's conscience. Without these ingredients the spirit of the hunt disappears. The animal's behavior is wholly inspired by the conviction that his life is at stake, and if it turns out that this is a complete fiction, that it is only a matter of taking his picture, the hunt becomes a farce and its specific tension evaporates. All of hunting becomes spectral when a photographic image, which is an apparition, is substituted for the prey. The use of a camera is comprehensible when it faces a pretty girl, a Gothic tower, a soccer goalie, or Einstein's hair; it is hopelessly inadequate when it faces the friendly wild boar rooting around in the thicket. The mannerism consists in treating the beast as a complete equal, and it seems to me more authentically refined and more genuine to accept the inevitable inequality which regulates and stylizes the perennial fact of hunting as sport.

One should not look for perfection in the arbitrary, because in that dimension there is no standard of measure; nothing has proportion nor limit, everything becomes infinite, monstrous, and the greatest exaggeration is at once exceeded by another. The Englishman probably believes he has reached the height of tenderness in substituting the camera for the rifle. Consider this, however. Because the waters of India are infectious, he took the filter there to purify them. With surprise he discovered that the Hindu, so remiss in adopting English customs, for once concurred with him and adopted the filter enthusiastically. This is a fine example of how two deeds that are externally identical can have opposite human motivation. While the Englishman used the filter to avoid being killed by microbes in the water, the Hindu, to whom death was unimportant, used it to avoid killing the microbes in the water with his own microbes or gastric juices. The incontinent tenderness of the Englishman is, without further ado, canceled out, but that does not guarantee any authentic superiority on the part of the Hindu. With no standard nothing has merit, and man is capable of using even sublimity to degrade himself.

In situations like the one just mentioned, the Englishman could learn that if he kills a bull his action has a meaning in no way similar to the meaning of killing a bull in a bullfight. Human activities cry out to be looked at from within, and if they almost always go so badly it is because, though they are so precise, we insist on looking at them in such an imprecise way and, when we can, with the naked eye only. If you try to stretch someone's comprehension a bit he will tell you that you are dealing in subtleties, instead of attending only to the question of whether or not the subtleties are true. It will seem a subtlety that after all I have said I should try to determine here the role that death plays in hunting as sport.

I have indicated that a sport is the effort which is carried out for the pleasure that it gives in itself and not for the transitory result that the effort brings forth. It follows that when an activity becomes a sport, whatever that activity may be, the hierarchy of its values becomes inverted. In utilitarian hunting the true purpose of the hunter, what he seeks and values, is the death of the animal. Everything else that he does before that is merely a means for achieving that end, which is its formal purpose. But in hunting as a sport this order of means to end is reversed. To the sportsman the death of the game is not what interests him; that is not his purpose. What interests him is everything that he had to do to achieve that death—that is, the hunt. Therefore what was before only a means to an end is now an end in itself. Death is essential because without it there is no authentic hunting: the killing of the animal is the natural end of the hunt and that goal of hunting itself, not of the hunter. The hunter seeks this death because it is no less than the sign of reality for the whole hunting process. To sum up, one does not hunt in order to kill; on the contrary, one kills in order to have hunted. If one were to present the sportsman with the death of the animal as a gift he would refuse it. What he is after is having to win it, to conquer the surly brute through his own effort and skill with all the extras that this carries with it: the immersion in the countryside, the healthfulness of the exercise, the distraction from his job, and so on and so forth.

In all of this, the moral problem of hunting has not been resolved, although it must be taken into account. We have not reached ethical perfection in hunting, not in the least. One never achieves perfection in anything, and perhaps it exists precisely so that one can never achieve it, as happens with cardinal points. Its purpose is to orient our conduct and to allow us to measure the progress accomplished. In this sense the advancement achieved in the ethics of hunting is undeniable. Therefore it is necessary to oppose photographic hunting, which is not progress but rather a digression and a prudery of hideous moral style.

Every authentic refinement must leave intact the authenticity of the hunt, its essential structure, which is a matter of a confrontation between two unequal species. The real care that man must exercise is not in pretending to make the beast equal to him, because that is a stupid utopia, a beatific farce, but rather in avoiding more and more the excess of his superiority. Hunting is the free play of an inferior species in the face of a superior species. That is where one must make some refinement. Man must give the animal a "handicap," in order to place him as close as possible to his own level, without pretending an illusory equivalence which, even if it were possible, would annihilate *ipso facto* the very reality of the hunt. Strictly speaking, the essence of sportive hunting is not raising the animal to the level of man, but something much more spiritual than that: a conscious and almost religious humbling of man which limits his superiority and lowers him toward the animal.

I have said "religious," and the word does not seem excessive to me. As I have already pointed out, a fascinating mystery of Nature is manifested in the universal fact of hunting: the inexorable hierarchy among living beings. Every animal is in a relationship of superiority or inferiority with regard to every other.* Strict equality is exceedingly improbable and anomalous. Life is a terrible conflict, a grandiose and atrocious confluence. Hunting submerges man deliberately in that formidable mystery and therefore contains something of religious rite and emotion in which homage is paid to what is divine, transcendent, in the laws of Nature.

---

* This permits order in the zoological existence. The species form groups in which the hunters and the hunted are articulated. They need each other in order to regulate themselves in the whole. There are no solitary species. More important than the collectivity of individuals is the collectivity of species. Any external intervention, if it is not done carefully, disarranges the marvelous clock of their coexistence. For example; in the game reserves created in Umfolozi, Mkuze, and elsewhere (Zululand), a grave diminishing in number of almost all species for lack of grazing had been observed. This scarcity was due to the fact that the herds of zebras and gnus or jackasses, all great grazers, had grown excessively. But at the same time this abnormal increase in gnus and zebras was due to the fact that hunters had killed too many of the beasts that had previously consumed a suitable number of zebras and gnus.

Hunting
and
Reason

ow that we have been looking at the hunt from within for a good while, now that we have learned the anatomy of its mesenteries, now that we have, in short, a sufficiently saturated vision of that reality, we can determine what role reason plays in man's form of hunting. For, of course, reason intervenes, as it does in all of man's other activities; the question is how and how much.

The traditional formula that man is a rational being has almost always been poorly understood, and this limited understanding has caused not only grave errors in theory, but also very grave errors in practice. It has always induced man to have extravagant illusions about himself. In fact, that phrase, like all those that do not limit themselves, invites us to understand it by taking its words in the fullness of their meaning. In this case, for example, we are to understand that man, hardly having begun to be a man, already had at his disposal, almost in its entirety, that power which we call "reason." Thus understood, that formula constitutes a crass error. It is false to assume that early man possessed, in any adequate sense of the word, the faculty of reason; he had of it only seeds and attempts, which have been developed throughout history, very gradually, by means of hard work, and in spite of immense setbacks. This is true to such an extent that, at the present moment, when man has lived about a million years on the planet, he is still fabulously far from a sufficient rationality. As the theologians used to say about another matter, man is *in via*; he is on the road to becoming rational—nothing more. To say, then, that man is rational is something like saying that the neighbor from Castuera is a Madrilenian because he took a train for Madrid. And the same thing happens with all the other specific attributes of humanity. If we really understood what rectifying this old formula involved, perhaps all aspects of our destiny would go better. But there is no opportunity to stop for this topic now. The important thing is to realize that man's rationality can only be measured with an eyedropper, and that one must count off very few drops for primitive man.

In order to subsist, this early man had to dedicate himself wholly to hunting. Hunting was, then, the first occupation, man's first work and craft. It is exceedingly important to remember this. The venatory occupation was unavoidable and practically the only one,* and as the center and root of existence it ruled, oriented, and organized human life completely—its acts and its ideas, its technology and sociality. Hunting was, then, the first *form of life* that man adopted, and this means—it should be fundamentally understood—that *man's being consisted first in being a hunter*. If we imagine our species to have disappeared at that point, the word "man" would lack meaning. Instead of calling that creature "man," we would have to call him "the hunter." Since he did not disappear, and for that central occupation were substituted others no less central, a more general term became necessary, one that would encompass infinite ways of being, innumerable forms of life. The capacity to be, one after another, an infinite number of different things, without one single imaginable thing being excluded on principle from the realm of possibility, is the true significance of the word "man."

Primitive hunting, however, was not a pure invention of primitive man. He had inherited it from the primate animal from which the human peculiarity sprang. Do not forget that man was once a beast. His carnivore's fangs and canine teeth are unimpeachable evidence of this. Of course he was also a vegetarian, like the Ovidae, as his molars attest. Man, in fact, combines the two extreme conditions of the mammal, and therefore he goes through life vacillating between being a sheep and being a tiger.

---

* One cannot doubt that early man had some complementary food from roots, tubers, and wild fruits. Perhaps in some regions he stole honey from the bees. But none of this probably signified much or became a formalized occupation; if it had it would have left some trace.

But Nature makes a leap between the pure beast that was the anthropoid and the rough outline of humanity that was the first Paleolithic man. Because Nature, about whom it has been said so many times that *"non facit saltus"*—she does not leap [jump]—has done almost nothing but jump. Today the doctrine of mutation—that is, of an evolution through leaps—opposes the doctrine of an evolution through continuity.

But we should imagine this early man as being still very close to the animal. He differs from the animal in that he has lost some instincts, or, which is the same thing, they have become dulled. On the other hand, he possesses a greater degree of memory and of that which is the inverse of memory: fantasy. He gathers and organizes more impressions, more experiences, than the pure beast, and this permits him to create more imaginative combinations, more intimate phantasmagoria, which give him an "interior life" denied to the animal.* The role of instinct is to direct behavior automatically. In this early man who was still the last animal, when an instinct failed and the poor being found himself not knowing what to do, fantasy prepared and delivered the image of a possible action. The fantastic projections of behavior were dull and stupid. But because he had to try so many, some proved useful and remained fixed as prodigious acquisitions. This and little more was early man's reason. As such it was a mere supplement to deficient instinct. Fortunately the greater part of his instincts remained active. He was still principally a beast. With the minimal dosage of reason he then possessed he would not have been able to shift for himself in life. This reason acted only here and there, like an orthopedic device imposed on a broken instinct. Without it man would have fallen below the animal. With it he succeeded in strictly maintaining himself above the animal's level at a distance no greater than that which generally exists between one zoological species and another. *Reason in primitive man has almost the same radius of action as instinct and in terms of its effects on the vital economy*

---

* See Wolfgang Köhler, *The Mentality of Apes* (New York: Harcourt, Brace, 1927), on this concrete point of the anthropoid's deficient memory.

** The instruments of flint which pertain to the pre-Chellean and Chellean periods do not greatly exceed the capacity to create instruments that Köhler (*op. cit.*), has demonstrated for the chimpanzee. Remember that calling primitive culture "the stone age" is a little arbitrary. Early man probably manipulated wood before, and more than, stone, and that is what the higher apes—chimpanzee, gorilla, and orangutan—principally employ in

should be considered as one more instinct, which takes the place of those which have been lost. **

Clearly, then, early Paleolithic man, the oldest that we know and the one who by chance was the hunter *par excellence*, was a man while still an animal. His reason was not sufficient to permit him to transcend the orbit of zoological existence: he was an animal intermixed with discontinuous lucidities, a beast whose intellect glowed from time to time in his intimate darkness. Such was the original, primordial way of being a man.

In these conditions he hunted. All the instincts that he still had played a part in his task, but in addition he employed thoroughly all his reason. This is the only form of hunting, among all those that man has practiced, which can truly be called a "reasoned pursuit." It can be called that precisely because it was not very reasoned. Nevertheless, the first traps were invented in that period. From the first, man was a very tricky animal. And he invented the first venatory stratagems: for example, the battue, which drove the game toward a precipice. The early weapons were insufficient for killing the free animal. Hunting was either forcing the game over a cliff or capturing it in traps or with nets and snares. Once the prey was caught it was beaten to death. Obermaier thinks that sometimes it was suffocated with clouds of smoke.

Starting from this outline we must conceive the later development. To do that it is necessary to think along two lines at once. Reason grows stronger. Man invents more and more effective weapons and techniques. In this direction man grows further away from the animal, raising his level above that of the beast. But along parallel lines, the atrophy of his instincts increases also and he grows away from his pristine intimacy with Nature. From being essentially a hunter he passes to being essentially a shepherd—that is, to a semistationary way of life. Very soon, he turns from shepherd into farmer, which is to say that he becomes completely stationary. The use of his legs, his lungs, his senses of smell, of orientation, of the winds, of the trails, all diminish. Normally, he ceases to be an expert tracker. This reduces his advantage over the animal; it maintains him in a limited range of superiority that permits the equation

making tools. The absence of wood tools in Paleolithic deposits is due to the perishable nature of vegetal material.

of the hunt. As he has perfected his weapons he has ceased to be wild—
that is, he has lost *form* as a fieldsman. The man who uses a ride today
does not generally live continuously on plains or in forests; rather he goes
there only for a few days. Today's best-trained hunter cannot begin to
compare his form to that of the sylvan actions of the present-day pygmy
or his remote counterpart Paleolithic man. Thus progress in weaponry is
somewhat compensated by regression in the form of the hunter.

The admiration and generous envy that some modern hunters feel
toward the poacher stems from this. The poacher is, in distant likeness, a
Paleolithic man—the municipal Paleolithic man, the eternal troglodyte
domiciled in modern villages. His greater frequenting of the mountain
solitudes has re-educated a little the instincts that have only a residual
nature in urban man. This reconfirms the idea that hunting is a confrontation between two systems of instincts. The poacher hunts better than
the amateur, not because he is more rational, but because he tires less, he
is more accustomed to the mountains, he sees better, and his predatory
instincts function more vigorously. The poacher always smells a little
like a beast, and he has the eyesight of a fox, a marten, or a field mouse.
The sporting hunter, when he sees a poacher at work in the field, discovers that he himself is not a hunter, that in spite of all his efforts and
enthusiasm he cannot penetrate the solid profundity of venatory knowledge and skill that the poacher possesses. It is the superiority of the professional, of the man who has dedicated his entire life to the matter, while
the amateur can only dedicate a few weeks of the year to it. We must
immerse ourselves wholly and heroically in an occupation in order to
dominate it, to *be* it!

Very soon reason reaches a degree of development that permits human
life to go beyond the horizon of the animal; thus, when man's superiority
becomes almost absolute, the role of reason in the hunt becomes inverted.
Instead of being used fully and directly in the task, it intervenes rather
obliquely and gets in its own way. Adult reason directs itself to tasks
other than hunting. When it does bother with the hunt, it pays most
attention to preliminary or peripheral questions. It will seriously endeav-
or to improve the species by scientific means, to select the breeds of
dogs, to dictate good laws for the hunt, to organize the game preserves,
and even to produce weapons which, *within very narrow limits*, will be

more accurate and effective. But one idea presides over all this: that the inequality between hunter and hunted should not be allowed to become excessive; reason will try to preserve the distance that existed between them at the beginning of history and, where possible, to improve it in favor of the animal. On the other hand, when the moment of the hunt actually arrives, reason does not intervene in any greater degree than it did in primitive times, when it was no more than an elemental substitute for the instincts. This clarifies the fact, incomprehensible from any other point of view, that the general lines of the hunt are identical today with those of five thousand years ago.

Vacations from the Human Condition

*T*hus the principle which inspires hunting for sport is that of *artificially perpetuating, as a possibility for man, a situation which is archaic in the highest degree: that early state in which, already human, he still lived within the orbit of animal existence.*

It is possible that I may have offended some hunter who presumes that my definition of hunting implies that I have treated him as an animal. But I doubt that any real hunter will be offended. For all the grace and delight of hunting are rooted in this fact: that man, projected by his inevitable progress away from his ancestral proximity to animals, vegetables, and minerals—in sum, to Nature—takes pleasure in the artificial return to it, the only occupation that permits him something like a vacation from his human condition. Thus the meditation which unfolds in the preceding pages has gone full circle, returning us to its beginning, because it means that when man hunts he succeeds in di-verting himself and in distracting himself from being a man. And this is the superlative diversion: it is the fundamental di-version. I am sorry if the reader has reached this final stage of our study tired out, but the truth is that the worst is yet to come.

To say "life" is the same as saying "here and now," because life is that which we must do here and now. That which we must do will vary a great deal in the diverse periods of history, but whatever it is, what never changes is that it is never done, rather we have yet to do it. Life is, then, essentially a task and an open problem—a tangle of problems that must be resolved, in the stormy plot of which, like it or not, we flail about shipwrecked. Lives which are not present—past lives—are not, of course, life in the proper sense of the word: they are stories that are told us about lives that once existed, that were problems for those who had to live them, as we have to live ours, before anyone could relate them. Thus in one aspect every life, while it is being lived, is more or less full of anguish, because it is a matter of unsolved problems urgently needing solutions. On the other hand, every time man looks at a past life from his perspective of the present, he sees, alongside the problems that weighed upon it, the solutions which, for better or for worse, these problems received. And so it naturally seems that every past life was easier, less full of anguish, than the present life; it is a charade whose solution we possess beforehand. Its problems have ceased to be open and therefore have ceased to be truly problems: the solution has closed them on themselves. That other life appears complete compared with the present life which is, by definition, always incomplete.

But, in addition, the venerable idea that

> *to our eyes*
> *any past time*
> *was better,* *

is not, perforce, arbitrary or obedient to an optical illusion from which the subject suffers; rather it possesses a solid foundation. With some exceptions which, when analyzed, only confirm the rule, it happens that, in truth, any past life was better, in the sense that it was less problematic, easier. If those past problems were of the same caliber as ours, we could take advantage, without further ado, of the solutions provided. Then it would be possible to inscribe our existence within the orbit of antiquity, with the advantage of already having, thanks to that past, our problematic situation resolved through anticipation. That is to say, history would be stabilized; life would have lost its dramatic substance of open enigma and unanswered urgency; over the planet there would have surged a reality radically different from life, with opposite characteristics—to wit, beatitude.

---

* Jorge Manrique, "*Coplas por la muerte de su padre*" [Verses on the death of his father.]

But the truth turns out to be the opposite of all this. What is normal is that the new life overflows the dimensions of the old. The doctrine of progress is false because it refers to the future and is blindly sure that man will always progress with astronomical inevitability, but if we eradicate its incontinence of prediction and turn it toward the past, it is strictly true and states an evident fact. In spite of one or another partial regression, human life has done nothing but progress, for better or for worse, at least in the unique sense that interests us here of having progressed in the complication of its obligations or problems. Seen from any "today," every past life exhibits an aspect of greater ease, not only because its solutions and results are already known, like a novel that one has read, but also because its problems are evidently simpler, and later man dominates them with superabundant elasticity.

This is the reason why man, submerged in the greater complexity of his present existence, normally feels nostalgia for the past, and even more for humanity's past than for his own individual past. When the forms of life practiced by our ancestors recede and pass on, they draw present-day men as if the forms wished to repossess the men. The past engenders the strong undertow of a low tide, and we must grasp the present well so that it does not drag us down and absorb us. For the past is a voluptuous siren. It has "sex appeal."

There is no period in which this nostalgia for other past times has not existed, because there has never been a period in which man felt that he had more than enough energy to deal with his own troublesome situation. He has always lived with the water at his throat. The past is a promise of greater simplicity for him: it seems to him that he could move with greater comfort and prepotency in those less-evolved forms of primitive life. Life would be a game for him. Of course, if he were actually transported by magic to that former way of life he would discover that it was not enough for him. Man is condemned to an inability to be substantively happy if he cannot be happy in the style of his own time. In the end, no period seriously and determinedly wants to emigrate away from itself, to exchange itself for another, and in this sense it can be said, although it may seem incredible at times, that every epoch is happy. But by the same token that there is no justification for posing the question of really emigrating to another age, so we have no defense against the constant appeal that the past makes to us to abandon the complications of the present and to save ourselves in it as if on an enchanted island.*

It is surprising to see the insistence with which all cultures, upon imagining a golden age, have placed it at the beginning of time, at the most primitive point. It was only a couple of centuries ago that the tendency to expect the best from the future began to compete with that retrospective illusion. Our hearts vacillate between a yearning for novelties and a constant eagerness to turn back. But in history the latter predominates. Happiness has generally been thought to be simplicity and primitivism. How happy man feels when he dreams of stripping off the oppressive present and floating in a more tenuous and simpler element! That is the obstinate dream of a "golden age"—that is, an "age of beginning"—whose delightful phantasmagoria emerges before the eyes of Don Quixote, as if from seeds, from some shriveled acorns he holds in his emaciated hand and which serve as a pretext for charming the goatherds with one of his most melodious orations.**

But there is no possible evasion. Man cannot return to any previous age. He is assigned, like it or not, to a future that is always, in fact, new and different, whether or not it is called progress. In spite of our species' age and our inheritance of all the past, life is always new and each generation finds itself obligated to begin the act of living, almost as if no one had ever done it before.

But since it is inadmissable to completely transfer our existence to a previous form of life, why not do so partially for a while, in order to rest from the painful existence of the here and now? This would be the great di-version.

Let us see what I can do for you. Where do you want to go? Do you want to be a good bourgeois of Versailles, one of Plutarch's men, a sixteenth-century Spanish hidalgo, a Christian in the style of Saint

---

* This hackneyed metaphor performs a useful service here. When men of an advanced civilization find themselves in a grave crisis—war, revolution—they dream about desert islands. This has happened to an incredible number of Spaniards first, and of other Europeans later, during the tragedies of these years [1936–1942]. This sudden epidemic of imaginary insularity and hysterical "Robinson-Crusoe-ism" is the comic note that is never missing from the tragedy. The occurrence has been so frequent that some reflections on it were unavoidable.

** Cervantes, *Don Quixote*, Book I, chapter XI.—Trans.

Augustine, a Celtiberian or Tarragonian Spaniard? The list of *desiderata* is immense. But do not bother to choose. You cannot be any of these for even a minute. Any attempt to bring it off will end, at best, in an unsatisfactory farce, a masquerade. Even to be a Christian you must be one on your own account and in today's style, which is not an easy job.

Those forms of life which have been produced in historical evolution were sustained by determinate conditions which cannot reoccur. Each one of them is inexorably tied to the date on which it arose, because it is the way of life invented by man *in view* of the way that immediately preceded him. Saint Augustine was a Christian in the style of someone who had just ceased to be a pagan and a disciple of Neoplatonism. Right there you have two of the innumerable suppositions implied in "being Christian in the style of Saint Augustine." As history advanced, the ways of being a man became more conditioned—we would say more "specialized." On the other hand, if we move backward, toward more and more elemental styles of life, specialization diminishes and we find more generic ways of being a man, with so few suppositions that, in *principle*, those ways would be possible or almost possible in any time; that is, they exist as *permanent availabilities in man*.

This is the reason men hunt. When you are fed up with the troublesome present, with being "very twentieth century," you take your gun, whistle for your dog, go out to the mountain, and, without further ado, give yourself the pleasure during a few hours or a few days of being "Paleolithic." And men of all eras have been able to do the same, without any difference except in the weapon employed. It has always been at man's disposal to escape from the present to that pristine form of being a man, which, because it is the first form, has no historical suppositions. History begins with that form. Before it, there is only that which never changes: that which is permanent, Nature. "Natural" man is always there, under the changeable historical man. We call him and he comes—a little sleepy, benumbed, without his lost form of instinctive hunter, but, after all, still alive. "Natural" man is first "prehistoric" man—the hunter.

The term "Paleolithic" is deplorable. It qualifies a certain form of human life by the instruments which it used and which, thanks to the resistance of their material, have come down to us. Prehistory, a science in the process of gestation, is dependent on the little data it has on the origins of humanity. Of those early lives it has hardly anything except things, and it is forced to classify life styles by the style of the objects used, or, what is even more absurd, by the materials: stone, copper, bronze, iron. But it is clear that a form of humanity can be suitably named only by its occupations, and, above all, by the central occupation that organizes and regulates all others. Thus the true meaning of the term "Paleolithic being" is "hunter." This was the essential fact of his condi-tion—not that he hunted with more or less polished stones. Then, and *only then*, living was hunting. Later, innumerable men hunted, but none has been fundamentally—that is, exclusively—a hunter.* On the other hand, with one difficulty or another, any man has been able to suspend for some time his real and authentic being and dedicate himself during that time to being a "hunter" in an artificial way. I can find no more ade-quate way of expressing the strange situation of historical man—present man, for example—when he occupies himself with hunting. How is such an enormous anachronism possible?

For we are not sufficiently surprised by the exceptional nature of this possibility. Perhaps this is because we assume, with erroneous negli-gence, that it is easy for us to effect in ourselves any past form of exis-tence. But this is false. As I have said, such an intention achieves only a fiction, a farce. But by hunting man succeeds, in effect, in annihilating all historical evolution, in separating himself from the present, and in renewing the primitive situation. An artificial preparation is necessary, certainly, for hunting to be possible. It is even necessary for the state to intervene, protecting the preserves or imposing the closed seasons with-out which there would be no game. But let us not confuse artifice with fiction: what is artificial in hunting remains prior to, and outside of, hunting itself. When, within that scope of conditions which artifice has imposed, modern man sets out to hunt, what he does is not a fiction, not a

---

* There were, and continue to be, surviving Paleolithics—that is, men who have never ceased to be hunters. The chronic nature of these ancient forms of life, or what is the same thing, the extravagant fact that "savages" exist today, is one of the least explained questions in existence. Let it be said so that we may be ashamed. The "sav-age" is the living fossil. On the other hand, as I have already indicated, prehistorians are gradually recognizing, against their will, that before the stone age there must have been a "wood age," which for obvious reasons has left no remains.

farce; it is, essentially, the same thing that Paleolithic man did. The only difference—doubtless decisive—is that for the latter hunting was the center of gravity for his whole life, while for the sportsman it is only a transitory suspension, almost parenthetical, of his authentic life. But that other creature which is going to occupy the parenthesis is also authentic. The duality which makes the situation so difficult to formulate is based on this. The hunter is, at one and the same time, a man of today and one of ten thousand years ago. In hunting, the long process of universal history coils up and bites its own tail.

When we leave the city and go up on the mountains it is astounding how naturally and rapidly we free ourselves from the worries, temper, and ways of the real person we were, and the savage man springs anew in us. Our life seems to lose weight and the fresh and fragrant atmosphere of an adolescence circulates through it. We feel (it is usually said) submerged in Nature. But the strange thing is that, although Nature is not our native or habitual environment, when the hunt places us in it we have the impression of returning to our old homestead. The hunting ground is never something exotic that we are discovering for the first time, but on the contrary something known beforehand, where we might have always been, and the savage man who suddenly springs up in us does not present himself as an unknown, as a novelty, but as our most spontaneous, evident, and comfortable being.

This is not just a vague observation. It sums up an infinite number of very precise facts. For example, take this description by a hunter* of a scene in which some hunters are going to a game reserve by car. Therefore, during the trip they do not bother to hunt. The rifles lie in their cases and sheaths. At this point two wolves cross the highway and with unusual tranquility stop a few yards from the vehicle. An intense tumult was instantly produced in each one of the travelers.

> *Braking, skidding, roars of "Where's my rifle?" "Give me my bullets!" Some jumped through a little door, others through a window....There was one enthusiast who, in the face of his inability to*

---

* Edward, Count Yebes, *Veinte Años de Caza Mayor* [Twenty Years a Big-Game Hunter] (Madrid, 1943).

get his rifle out of the sheath, thought seriously of pulling his knife and tearing the leather of the case.

Let us call things by their proper names; all that sudden uproar shows the automatic discharge of the predatory instinct which survives in modern man as a rudiment. In this case since the men are hunters, it means that the archaic and suffering instinct, nourished by exercise, has been notably rehabilitated in them.

But the reaction is typical, and it deserves close attention, because it constitutes the essential means without which hunting would not exist today and which was established in the organism of man hundreds of thousands of years before history began. The hunters, of course, see the two wolves as "game"—that is, as creatures with regard to which the only adequate behavior is to hunt them. It is a question of reflex and not of deliberation, not even for an instant. It is not man who gives to those wolves the role of possible prey. It is the animal—in this case the wolves themselves—which demands that he be considered in this way, so that to not react with a predatory intention would be antinatural. Let me explain this. Cattle raising is a relationship between man and animal that was invented by man and begins in him; if we were to represent it graphically we would have to draw an arrow that goes from man to the animal. This is not "livestock" in itself. It is a matter of a condition or "role" that man projects on the beast. But hunting, as I have already suggested in passing, is a relationship that certain animals impose on man, to the point where not trying to hunt them demands the intervention of our deliberate will. The graphic symbol for the hunting relationship would have to be the inverse of that which represents cattle raising; the arrow would have to be drawn emerging from the animal.

It should not be said, then, that the hunters in the scene described are exceptionally destructive beings that annihilate whatever comes into their view. Not at all; they see the wolves as what they really are—creatures gifted with marvelous powers of evasion, to the point where they are, essentially, "that which escapes," the unsubmissive, the surly, the fugitive, which is generally hidden, absent, unobtainable, wrapped in solitude. "To have the wolves there!" when the wolves are precisely "that which is not there!" All of which is the same as saying that wolves, by nature, count on an "ideal" hunter. Before any particular hunter pursues them they feel themselves to be possible prey, and they model their whole existence in terms of this condition. Thus they automatically convert any normal man who comes upon them into a hunter. *The only adequate response to a being that lives obsessed with avoiding capture is to try to catch it.* And the same thing that happens to the wolves happens to all other animals on the list of species that are associated with man in a hunting relationship. Any one of those that suddenly appears in the countryside provokes in us that typical surprise. The sudden flurry of a partridge behind a thicket generates that strange contraction of our nervous and circulatory systems, whose symptoms seem extraordinarily like fright, although they represent the opposite of fear, since they end in an automatic movement of pursuit.

This very humble reflex, residual fossil of an instinct that man retains from the time he was a pure beast, is the reason why today, at the end of uncountable millennia, he can make hunting a form of happiness. To distract and di-vert ourselves it is not enough always to be ready to abandon the laborious occupations of everyday life; it is also necessary that another way of life, another occupation, possess the gift of seizing us, of monopolizing our interest. Diversion has two poles: that *from* which we divert or remove ourselves and that *with* which we divert or absorb ourselves. We are always ready for the first; but the latter is the more difficult, the improbable. Because we lack it we often fall into those enigmatic chasms of vital emptiness that are generally called wearisomeness, "spleen," boredom.

Man is a fugitive from Nature. He escaped from it and began to make history, which is trying to realize the imaginary, the improbable, perhaps the impossible. History is always made against the grain of Nature. The human being tries to rest from the enormous discomfort and all-embracing disquiet of history by "returning" transitorily, artificially, to Nature in the sport of hunting. We are such paradoxical creatures that each day will require greater artifice to give us the pleasure of sometimes being "natural beings." But no matter how great and ingenious the artifice may be, it will be in vain if that ferocious instinct, already evanescent, is completely erased in our species.

This is the strongest reason I have for turning against photographic hunting. In it, that instinct is cheated and mocked, and thus its total extinction is encouraged. To its demand for real and tangible capture, which alone would satisfy it, man responds by carrying off an image of the animal, a view of it. What we call a "view," the Greeks called "an idea." This hunting is, in fact, idealistic hunting, platonic hunting, and Platonism represents the maximum tradition of affected piety.

No; we need to conserve that bitter impulse that we have inherited from primitive man. It alone permits us the greatest luxury of all, the ability to enjoy a vacation from the human condition through an authentic "immersion in Nature." But that immersion is not as easy to achieve as is usually supposed without thinking about it. Man cannot re-enter Nature except by temporarily rehabilitating that part of himself which is still an animal. And this, in turn, can be achieved only by placing himself in relation to another animal. But there is no animal, pure animal, other than the wild one, and the relationship with him is the hunt.

Thus contemplated, the fact that hunting has perpetually occupied the highest rank in the repertory of man's happinesses loses its surprising and even extravagant character.

It should be noticed that only by hunting can man *be in* the country; I mean *within* a countryside which, moreover, is authentically countryside. And only the hunting ground is true countryside. No other form is pure countryside—neither farmland, nor battleground, nor tourist country. As the expression indicates, *cultivated* countryside is land already exhausted by humanity to the point where that humanization of the countryside has served as model and name for all the more specifically human ways of life: *the culture.** To walk, then, through an orchard, sown field, or stubble field, through an olive grove laid out in diagonal rows or a methodically planned grove of pin oaks, is to follow man traveling within himself. The battlefield is similar. War, like agriculture, is a human institution. When it is used for battle the field converts a piece of the planet into a geometric area where only strategical conditions are important.

---

* Luis Vives [1492–1540] was the first to employ this denomination of cultivation in reference to literary and scientific occupations: *cultura animi* [culture of the spirit]. Later Bacon, clearly much influenced by Vives, speaks of *georgica mentis* [tillage of the mind].

Finally, for the tourist, the countryside, as landscape, is no less human than the others: it is a "painting" and its existence depends on the lyric conditions that man wishes and is able to mobilize. That is why it has taken so long for our species to be interested in it. Poets and painters are the ones who have formed it, little by little, and its qualities were discovered—that is, invented—slowly, generation by generation, in periods of very advanced culture. It is a pity that there does not exist a history of landscape, which signifies one of the greatest conquests and enrichments of historical man. To tell the truth, in Europe it was a romantic invention. Only by the beginning of the nineteenth century was there enough force behind the human impulse which leads man to convert a piece of ground into the ideality of a landscape.

But, in addition, countryside as landscape and mere spectacle makes us perceive with complete clarity what happens also, though less obviously, with farmland and battleground—to wit: that it remains before us, that we cannot enter into it, that we go on without being able to get outside of ourselves. Only on the hunting ground, which is the first countryside, the only "natural" one, can we succeed in emigrating from our human world to an authentic "outside," from which history represents the retreat or anabasis. But it is clear that we cannot get "outside" if we do not enter into that "outside," if we stay located and anchored in our habitual terrain. It is not for nothing that the words which in Indo-European languages signified "countryside" also meant "outside," and they are precisely those that meant "door." Countryside is that which is beyond our habitation, whether that is a house, a garden, a park, or a hacienda.

Only the wild animal is properly in the countryside, not just on top of it, simply having it in view. If we want to enjoy that intense and pure happiness which is a "return to Nature," we have to seek the company of the surly beast, descend to his level, feel emulation toward him, pursue him. This subtle rite is the hunt.

When one is hunting, the air has another, more exquisite feel as it glides over the skin or enters the lungs, the rocks acquire a more expressive physiognomy, and the vegetation becomes loaded with meaning. But all this is due to the fact that the hunter, while he advances or waits crouching, feels tied through the earth to the animal he pursues, whether the animal is in view, hidden, or absent.

The reader who is not a hunter may think that these last words are mere phraseology, simply a manner of speaking. But the hunter will not. They know very well that it is literally true: that when they are in the field the axis of the whole situation is that mystical union with the animal, a sensing and presentiment of it that automatically leads the hunter to perceive the environment from the point of view of the prey, without abandoning his own point of view. This is paradoxical in itself and appears to be contradictory, but it cannot be denied. After all, I am talking about an extremely simple matter: the pursuer cannot pursue if he does not integrate his vision with that of the pursued. That is to say, *hunting is an imitation of the animal.* Therefore we will not understand hunting if we take it as a human fact and not as a zoological fact that man takes delight in producing.

In that mystical union with the beast a contagion is immediately generated and the hunter begins to behave like the game. He will instinctively shrink from being seen; he will avoid all noise while traveling; he will perceive all his surroundings from the point of view of the animal, with the animal's peculiar attention to detail. This is what I call being within the countryside. Only when we see it through the drama that unfolds in the hunt can we absorb its particular richness. Articulated in that action which is a minor zoological tragedy, wind, light, temperature, ground contour, minerals, vegetation, all play a part; they are not simply there, as they are for the tourist or the botanist, but rather they *function*, they act. And they do not function as they do in agriculture, in the unilateral, exclusive, and abstract sense of their utility for the harvest, but rather each intervenes in the drama of the hunt from within itself, with its concrete and full being.

When he hunts, not only does man imitate the animal's generic integration, but a number of the fundamental hunting techniques are mimetic also. I have already referred to crouching and sneaking, to traveling silently.* But there is much more. The most primitive method of hunting, apart from trapping the animal or pushing it over a cliff, is that which consists in going toward the animal and getting as close to it as possible, and this is based on resembling the animal, disguising oneself

* Strictly speaking, these procedures were also learned from animals.

like it. In the cave paintings the deer hunter already appears covered with a deer skin, the antlers of the stag swinging on the human head. This had a more serious meaning for primitive man than it does for us, because his mental process, prior to and different from our abstractions, made him believe that what is similar is identical; that the image of a thing *is* the thing and that when man adopted the form of an animal he became that animal. The primitive that pretends to be a bison, wrapping himself in the skin and resting the formidable horns on the back of his head, is himself a bison. In the same way the present-day Central African savage is an ostrich when he walks along stooped over, carrying on his shoulders the erect neck and stupid head of an ostrich.*

* The imitation of the animal is so indigenous to hunting that the hunter does not notice it, as one does not notice the element in which one finds oneself. Count Yebes [*op. cit.*] in explaining the technique of deer hunting with decoy calls—a technique unknown in Spain, but often practiced in Central Europe—does not realize the comic aspect of the scene when he describes how, in a Bohemian forest during the height of the deer mating season, a great old gentleman, whom we recognize as an electoral prince of the Holy Roman Empire, or something only a little less venerable, instructs him in the procedure, and to this end rests his venerability on a tree trunk, puts a minuscule whistle to his lips, and surrenders himself to the task of imitating the prenuptial noises of a jealous doe.

The Hunter—
the Alert Man

evertheless, the particular ways in which the hunter imitates the game are secondary. They spring up against the background of a more radical imitation, which leads man to adopt the attitude of existence by which wild animals generally live and the abandonment of which constitutes precisely the characteristic of humanity.

As everyone knows, every well-informed rule only transforms the definition of an exemplary reality into an imperative. If someone says: to hunt well you should, first of all and above all, do such-and-such, we must understand that what is being said is: really and truly to hunt is to do that. Let me quote from the text of a fine hunter:

> *There is one of the hunter's senses which must work indefatigably at all times. That is the sense of sight. Look, look, and look again; at all times, in all directions, and in all circumstances. Look as you go along; look while you are resting; look while you are eating or lighting a cigar; up, down, back over the ground you have just covered, at the hill crests, at the ledges and dells, with binoculars and the naked eye, and always be aware that if you know how to look, the beast that you have not found in eight hours of backbreaking work can appear within a hundred meters, when just at sunset, worn out and cursing your interest, you are taking off your shoes and caring for your aching feet in the door of a shelter or a tent. It's good advice.**

* Yebes, *op. cit.*

It is not, then, walking and walking, climbing cliffs, going down into gullies and gorges, sneaking quietly, waiting patiently, or being a good shot that the hunter must essentially do, but rather—who would guess!— the least muscular of all operations: looking. But this hunting look on which the whole crude task of the hunt paradoxically depends is not, as is evident, any old look.

Merely to look, without reiteration or enhancement, is to direct the sight to a point in the surroundings where we suppose beforehand the object in question is. The radius of the look is projected by the attention, which seizes on that point, leaving the rest unattended. Our attention, which is what aims our vision, seizes on that spot on the horizon because we are persuaded that what interests us will appear there. This attention to the preconceived is equivalent to being absorbed in one point of the visible area and not paying attention to the other points.

The hunter's look and attention are completely opposite to this. He does not believe that he knows where the critical moment is going to occur. He does not look tranquilly in one determined direction, sure beforehand that the game will pass in front of him. The hunter knows that he does not know what is going to happen, and this is one of the greatest attractions of his occupation. Thus he needs to prepare an attention of a different and superior style—an attention which does not consist in riveting itself on the presumed but consists precisely in not presuming anything and in avoiding inattentiveness. It is a "universal" attention, which does not inscribe itself on any point and tries to be on all points. There is a magnificent term for this, one that still conserves all its zest of vivacity and imminence: alertness. The hunter is the alert man.

But this itself—life as complete alertness—is the attitude in which the animal exists in the jungle. Because of it he lives from within his environment. The farmer attends only to what is good or bad for the growth of his grain or the maturation of his fruit; the rest remains outside his vision and, in consequence, he remains outside the completeness that is the countryside. The tourist sees broadly the great spaces, but his gaze glides, it seizes nothing, it does not perceive the role of each ingredient in the dynamic architecture of the countryside. Only the hunter, imitating the perpetual alertness of the wild animal, for whom everything is danger, sees everything and sees each thing functioning as facility or difficulty, as risk or protection.

And this is how we can understand the extraordinary fact that, with maximum frequency, when a philosopher wanted to name the attitude in which he operated when musing, he compared himself with the hunter. "*Thereutes*," Plato says over and over again; Saint Thomas Aquinas repeats "*Venator*."

Notice, for example, how Plato in the *Republic* (432 B), trying to define justice—and for him defining is always like capturing the thing—embarks in depth and with *delectatio nervosa* [a thrill of delight] on the metaphor of the hunt:

> *SOCRATES: Now then, Glaucon, we must post ourselves (we philosophers) like a ring of huntsmen around the thicket, with very alert minds, so that justice does not escape us by evaporating before us. It is evident that it must be there somewhere. Look out then and do your best to get a glimpse of it before me and drive it toward me.*
> *GLAUCON: I only wish I could! It will be enough if I can see what you point out as you guide me.*
> *SOCRATES: Come on, then, I'll encourage you!*
> *GLAUCON: That I will, provided that you lead me.*
> *SOCRATES: Very well, but, by heaven! Look how obstructed and overgrown the woods are. What a dark and hard-to-see place! But there's nothing to do but go forward.*
> *GLAUCON: Let's go then!*
> *SOCRATES: By the devil! I think we have a track, and I don't think it will escape us now.*

This is, by the way, authentic proof that Plato himself had hunted. That passage could not have been written by a man who had not often been out in the woods obsessed with detecting prey. To translate this section exactly I had to use the most forceful terms of hunting slang, for example, "drive the game toward me"—literally, "press it against me." Note, furthermore, how often Socrates, pedagogue-hunter, tells Glaucon to look, look, look, and to be alert.

In fact, the only man who truly thinks is the one who, when faced with a problem, instead of looking only straight ahead, toward what habit, tradition, the commonplace, and mental inertia would make one assume, keeps himself alert, ready to accept the fact that the solution might spring from the least foreseeable spot on the great rotundity of the horizon.

Like the hunter in the absolute *outside* of the countryside, the philosopher is the alert man in the absolute *inside* of ideas, which are also an unconquerable and dangerous jungle. As problematic a task as hunting, meditation always runs the risk of returning empty-handed. Hardly anyone can fail to know the probability of this result if he has tried, as I have in these pages, to hunt down the hunt.